# HINDU IDOLATRY
AND
# ENGLISH ENLIGHTENMENT

# HINDU IDOLATRY

AND

# ENGLISH ENLIGHTENMENT

## SIX LETTERS

## ADDRESSED TO EDUCATED HINDUS

## CONTAINING A PRACTICAL DISCUSSION OF HINDUISM

W. HASTIE

GYAN

*Published by*

GYAN

Gyan Publishing House
5, Ansari Road
Daryaganj, New Delhi-110002
Phone: 011-47034999, 9811692060
E-mail: books@gyanbooks.com

*Distribution Network*
gyanbooks.com
India, USA, Canada, UK, Australia



ISBN: 978-93-6920-768-8 (HB)

First Published, 1883

2nd Impression 2025

*Printed at:* Gyan Press, Delhi.



**HINDU IDOLATRY AND ENGLISH ENLIGHTENMENT**
Author : W. HASTIE

# HINDU IDOLATRY

AND

# ENGLISH ENLIGHTENMENT.

SIX LETTERS

ADDRESSED TO EDUCATED HINDUS

CONTAINING A PRACTICAL DISCUSSION OF

HINDUISM.

BY

W. HASTIE, B. D.

Principal of the General Assembly's Institution,

Calcutta.

Calcutta:

THACKER, SPINK AND CO.

EDINBURGH : DAVID DOUGLAS.

1882.

For I am not ashamed of the Gospel of Christ: for it is the power of God unto salvation to every one that believeth; to the Jew first and also to the Greek. For therein is the righteousness of God revealed from faith to faith.—Romans, 1, 16.

Though I preach the Gospel, I have nothing to glory of: for necessity is laid upon me; yea, woe is unto me, if I preach not the Gospel!—I Cor. 9, 16.

To

THE EDUCATED HINDUS OF BENGAL,
From many of whom I have received much kindness,
and to all of whom, 'both to the wise and
to the unwise', 'I am debtor, so much as
in me is, to preach the Gospel,'

THESE LETTERS

ON THEIR RELATION TO THE POPULAR IDOLATRY,

ARE RESPECTFULLY ADDRESSED,

With the sincerest desire for their Good.

सुलभाः पुरुषा राजन् सततं प्रियवादिनः ।
अप्रियस्य तु पथ्यस्य वक्ता श्रोता च दुर्लभः ॥
यो हि धर्मं समाश्रित्य हित्वा भर्त्तुः प्रियाप्रिये ।
अप्रियाण्याह पथ्यानि तेन राजा सहायवान् ॥

MAHABHARATA, V. 1348—9.

Bland, courtly men are found with ease,
Who utter what they know will please ;
But honest men are far to seek,
Who bitter truths and wholesome speak.
So, too, those thoughtful men are rare
Who blunt and sound advice can bear.

A Prince's best ally is he,
The man from servile truckling free,
Who faithful counsel gives, nor fears
With truth to wound his patron's ears ;
Not he who spares him present pain
At certain cost of future bane.

*Dr. John Muir's Translation.*

## PREFATORY NOTE.

The following Letters were called forth by the incidental Report of a great Hindu ceremony; but so far from being the utterance of a merely accidental opinion, they express matured convictions which have only been strengthening during the course of my work and experience in India. Written rapidly in the midst of my daily avocation and as a part of it, the first five have just appeared in the columns of the *Statesman*, as the Editor could find opportunity for inserting them, a kindness which in its various relations I would again cordially acknowledge.

Although the subject of the Hindu Idolatry has been often discussed in a much more thorough and exhaustive manner, and although the more practical side of it remains for further consideration, it has been suggested to me by my Missionary Colleagues in the General Assembly's Institution and by other Members of the Mission Board of the Church of Scotland, that the discussion thus far, might be reprinted, at this time, even in its original popular form, not only to make it more accessible to the educated Hindus whose spiritual well-being is our common care, but as likely to be of interest to the friends of our educational Missions by shewing them the position with which we have practically to deal. It is the former consideration that has chiefly weighed with me, and, accordingly, I now send forth these Letters on a wider mission of appeal to the intelligence and conscience of the educated men of Bengal, who are at once our anxiety and our hope ; and not without some anticipation of the same kindly reception as my views have always received from my own Students. They go from me in prayerful dependence upon the Divine blessing which is often poured most abundantly upon the humblest offering, and with a sincere acknowledgment of their imperfection, incompleteness, and inadequacy for the great end in view : but, withal, from a Faith that is perfect in its Object, a Hope that is complete in its expectation of Divine triumph, and a Love that is at least adequate to bear the reproach of its own infirmity, while waiting through the strong Son of God who was Love Itself, for that Diviner forgiveness, which is ever ready in Him, "to make allowance for us all."

W. H.

The General Assembly's Institution.
October 20, 1882.

## CONTENTS.

# A SHRADH CEREMONY

## IN THE

# SOBHA BAZAAR RAJBAREE.

———oo———

*Report reprinted from the Statesman of September 20, 1882.*

———oo———

THE *shradh* ceremony or *requiem* service of the Dowager Maharanee, widow of the late Maharaja Kali Krishna Bahadoor, and grandmother of the Maharaja Harendra Krishna Bahadoor, was held last Sunday morning.

It was performed in the spacious quadrangle of the *rajbaree*—one of the largest in Calcutta. The quadrangle was very tastefully and elaborately decorated under the superintendence of the well-known engineer, Baboo Mohindro Chunder Bose, and presented the unusual spectacle of a stately *danshagur*, consisting of sixteen sets of beds, sixteen sets of silver plates and utensils, the plates of each separate set bearing a thousand rupees in silver. There were, besides, with each set, shawls, broadcloth, tusser silk, and silk *dhooties* and *chudders*. These articles were all arranged on the east side of the quadrangle ; on the south were heaps of brass utensils of every description, symmetrically arranged, together with a *palki* and horse.

On the daïs was a satin *musnud*, on which was a set of silver *utterdhan*, *golabpash* and *phooldhan*. As a canopy over the daïs was a silver umbrella, and on one side a silver *punkah*.

All these were dedicated to the service of the family idol, *Gopinathjee*, who was brought and placed on a silver throne over the *musnud* to hallow the service with his sacred presence. Nearly four thousand *Adyapaks*, or professors of Hindoo logic, philosophy, law, rhetoric, and literature, were invited to the convocation from the principal *tols* or educational institutions of Bengal, Behar, and Orissa. Besides these, invitations were issued among sixteen hundred of the Maharaja's friends and acquaintances in different parts of Bengal, of whom 482 were of the *Kyast* caste; while delegates from several distant quarters helped to swell the number. The hour fixed for the service was 8 A.M., and by that time the streets in the vicinity of the *rajbaree*, as well as Raja Nobo Kissen's-street, presented a scene of animation and bustle, which several European and native constables of the Reserve Force, specially detailed for the work, could with difficulty control. Amongst the principal *Kulins*, there were representatives from the following ancient and respectable families, namely, the Bose family of Khanakoll, Kristonagar, the Rai Saheb Mitters of Dacca, the Mitters of Koomartolee, Durzipara, Chore Bagan, Soora, Baksha, Hooghly, Howrah, Joynuggur, and Muzilpore; the Surbadhicaries of Sham Bazaar and Potoldanga; the Ghoses of Jorasanko, Simla, and Cornwallis-square; the Bose Mullicks of Potoldanga and Cantapookur, Combooliatola, and Baug Bazaar. Amongst the *Mauliks* there were present members of the Dutt families of Nimtollah and Wellington-square; the Singhs of Jorasanko; the Paulits of Dingabhanga, Entally; the Goohos of Hoogulkooria, and the Roys of Narail, &c. Besides the above, who were the principal guests of the day, there were present Maharaja the Hon'ble Sir Jotindro Mohun Tagore, K.C.S.I., Raja Rajendra Narain Deb, Raja Rajendra Mullick, Raja Poorna Chunder Singh, Koomar Indur Chunder Singh, Baboo Koonjolall Bannerjee, Baboo Charoo Chunder Mullick, Baboo Denonath Mullick, Rai Shama Churn Day, Bahadoor, Hon'ble Doorga Churn Law, Hon'ble Kristodas Pal, Dr. Rajendralala Mitra, Baboo Tarini Churn Bose, Baboo Doyal Chunder Dutta, Baboo Satkory Mitter, Baboo Gonesh Chunder Chunder, Baboo Kali Kissen Tagore's eldest son, Baboo Sarutindro Mohun Tagore, Rai Jadub Chunder Ghose, Bahadoor, Rai Kanai Lall Dey, Bahadoor, Baboo Jodoolal Mullick, Baboo Damoodar Dass Barman, Rai Hurropersad Chowdry, Baboo Moorally Dhur Sen, Baboo Kallynath Mitter, Baboo Woodoy Chand Bose, Baboo Oorono Prokash Gangooly, Baboo Troyluckho Nath Mitter, Baboo Unnoda Prosad Bannerjee, Rai Juggodanund Mookerjee, Bahadoor, Baboo Mohendro Nath Bose, Baboo Obhoy Churn Gooho, Baboo Prankissen Mookerjee, Baboo Pertab Chunder Ghose, Baboo Rama Nath Law, and others. The company having been seated, Raja Harendra Krishna, being the eldest of the Maharanee's grandchildren, obtained leave, with folded arms, according to Hindoo custom, from Maharaja Komul Krishna Bahadoor, as the head of the family, to perform the *shradh* ceremony. The Maharaja, before according permission, had himself to obtain the leave of the convocation. During the performance of the service, which lasted about half-an-hour, the whole assembly remained standing. The Vedic benediction having been pronounced by all the Brahmins present in a body, the assembly slowly dispersed. In the evening some ten to twelve thousand beggars received charity in the shape of small coin. On the second day over 2,000 Brahmins were feasted ; on the third day the *Kaysts* had a feast ; while some 3,500 ladies partook of a banquet on the fourth day. The fifth and last day, the tenants and domestics were entertained.

The ceremonials were under the direction of Maharaja Komal Krishna Bahadoor, who has obtained his experience of the management of these and similar Hindoo ceremonies from the late Maharaja Sir Radha Kant, his Cousin, and his brother, Maharaja Kali Krishna Bahadoor, who like himself were the acknowledged heads—*Ghosti-poti*—of the Hindoo community.

Many and numerous were the letters of condolence received by Maharaja Harendra Krishna Bahadoor. We publish two only—the first from his Highness the Maharaja of Travancore, G.C.S.I., and the second from his Highness the Maharaja of Doomraon. His Highness the Maharaja of Travancore says : "My dear Raja Harendra Krishna, Bahodoor,—

It has grieved me exceedingly to hear of the demise of your dear and honoured grandmother. But it is a source of satisfaction to you and all your friends that she died so full of years, amidst her worthy and affectionate children, and attended with all the observances prescribed in your holy *Shastras*. You will accept my sincere sympathy on this sad occasion. Death has been busy in our family, too. I lost my eldest brother a week ago, aged 55." His Highness the Maharaja of Doomraon writes: "My dear Maharaja Harendra Krishna,—It grieves me much to hear that the celebrated old lady of Calcutta, your grandmother, has ceased to live, and that according to our holy *Shastras* she has been able to breathe her last on the banks of the Ganges (Hooghly) while reciting the name of her God. It is my prayer to Him that she may abide in eternal happiness in heaven. To die is the lot of humanity, so it is needless for me to tender you my condolence for the sad bereavement, while you have the satisfaction to know that she lived to the most mature age of 99 years, and has now left behind her such worthy children as yourselves. I wish, if it were not for the distance, I had been present, and joined with my friends in Calcutta in doing honor to her memory."

In conclusion, we may mention that a *shradh* ceremony on so grand and expensive a scale has not been known in Calcutta for many years.

---

# LETTERS

## ON

## THE SOBHA BAZAAR RAJBAREE SHRADH.

## I.

## THE MOST STRIKING FACTS OF THE SHRADH.

——*oo*——

### To the Editor.

Sir,—It appears, then, from your report of this splendid *shradh*, that the well-educated Maharaja Harendra Krishna Bahadoor still pays Divine honor to "the family idol *Gopinathjee*, who was brought and placed on a silver throne *to hallow the service with his sacred presence*." His Highness the Maharaja of Doomraon writes to say how sincerely he wished to join in the worship, but is consoled at a distance by the fact that "the celebrated old lady" was able to breathe her last on the banks of the Ganges "while reciting the name of her god." And the highly enlightened Maharaja of Travancore finds "a source of satisfaction"—as he puts it in his correct English—in the thought that the justly lamented Dowager Maharanee has had the benefit of "all the observances prescribed in the holy *shastras*." Nay, that learned modern scholar, Dr. Rajendralala Mitra, C.I.E., whom we all delight to honor, was present to grace the occasion, as the most conspicuous figure among "nearly 4,000 *Adyapaks* or professors of Hindoo logic, philosophy, law, rhetoric, and literature, from the principal *tols* or educational institutions of Bengal, Behar, and Orissa." And to crown the wonder, that most patriotic and progressive leader of young Bengal, the Hon'ble Kristo Das Pal—with Maharaja the Hon'ble Sir Jotindro Mohun Tagore, K.C.S.I., and a hundred more of "the observed of all observers" —was there as the representative of political and social reform to smile approval on this perfection of brahmanic ceremonialism, and on the indiscriminate charity of the noble mourners to "ten or twelve thousand beggars"! These facts alone, apart altogether from their rich and solemn setting in what Hamlet calls "the trappings and the suits of woe," are at the least extremely remarkable, and to any unprejudiced observer must suggest many grave practical reflections.

Sympathising sincerely as I do with the occasion of this imposing ceremony, I have of course not a word to say that would give the slightest pain to the mourners, or throw a shade over any real consolation that may have been drawn from the very "luxury of woe." Rather would I, in accordance with my proper duty, try only to bind up the broken hearts by pointing them to the Man of Sorrows, who is alone able to "wipe away all tears from our eyes," and to turn our earthly sorrow into eternal joy by inspiring the sure hope of that happier home where "there shall be no more death, neither sorrow, nor crying, neither shall there be any more pain." I have no intention even of reflecting upon the useless extravagance with which the pomp of this sorrowing grandeur was purchased, for no one could be inclined at the time to express disapprobation of any becoming form of mourning that might be consistent with the rank and wealth of such a highly-respected family. And I would be the last to write a word that would seem to discourage any patronage of literature and learning around us, or to check any generous outpouring of charity upon the more miserable and helpless constituents of native society. But your account of this very elaborate and gorgeous religious show, has forced upon me more irresistibly than ever a problem with which I am daily perplexed, and of which I would fain see some hope of practical solution. It is the problem of the relation of our English education and civilisation to the traditional Idolatry, and more particularly the question of the moral and personal responsibility of the educated and enlightened heads of the Hindoo community for its continued countenance and perpetuation. If we did not know it from experience, it would sound utterly incredible to be told that these cultivated and accomplished gentlemen, some of them Fellows of the Calcutta University and Members of learned European Societies, were found in the centre of this vast crowd on Sunday morning last, whose central purpose was the worshipping of what they at least knew to be but a gawky image gilded and adorned to attract the vulgar eye, but,—like Old Marley—"as dead as a door nail," and, happily on that account, incomparably less dangerous than the living god would have been, as we know from his history, to the virtue of the 3,500 ladies who partook of the banquet on the fourth day. It seems to me that the time has come for earnest expostulation with the respected leaders of the Hindu community upon this glaring evil ; nay, more, that the time has surely come, even with observation, for some practical action being taken by themselves in the matter which shall be at once consistent with their own dignity, the honour of their name, and the good of their country.

If you will allow me, I would fain make a few remarks in this direction out of a deep, sincere, constraining conviction that possesses me, as a friend of Hindu society and as a worker for its reformation. In doing so I shall carry with me all the breadth and tolerance of Christian charity, and shall look at the question in its general bearings rather than in individual details. But as I could not say even the little that is in my mind upon the subject, in a few words at the close of this letter, I shall pause to-day with merely raising the question, in the hope that you will let me return to it whenever my engagements permit me to lift my pen again for this purpose.

W. HASTIE.

The General Assembly's Institution,
September 21, 1882.

## II.

## THE SUPPOSED NECESSITY OF IDOLATRY.

### To the Editor.

Sir,—I shall not do the educated gentlemen, who publicly took part in this great *shradh*, the wrong of even entertaining the supposition that they are themselves really Idolators. If they were, I would have nothing to say to them in particular, as distinguished from their other countrymen, but would pursue my work in silence, with only the practical protest of the daily patience and hope of a higher faith. But it is just because I know that they are *not* inwardly sincere or true to themselves in any of their forms of idolatrous worship, and because I believe that this practical insincerity or unreality of theirs is sucking the life-blood out of the very hope of their community, that I venture to touch however slightly, upon this delicate subject. And because I further know them to be thoroughly open, on the intellectual side at least, to a full conviction of their practical duty in any matter whatever, I confidently anticipate that they will bear with me in anything I may now say from my own point of view, since it will be said with all earnestness and out of the deepest sympathy with their common desire for what is good.

I do not pretend to be an authority on the Hindu idolatry. I am, however, aware of the ingenious and clever and even scornful argumentation that would at once be unfolded, in noisy passages of ancient rhetoric, by those 4,000 Pundits, if they were only told of my antagonism. But I am also as sure as I could be of anything, that mere verbal ingenuity can never get over the patent and practical evils of the popular superstition, which no sophistry can defend, however charity may merely bewail them for a time. I shall not attempt even to mention all the various arguments that are advanced by educated men in defence of their participating in idolatrous ceremonies ; but, with your permission, I shall briefly glance at the one under which they all ultimately take shelter, and which practically covers all the rest.

It is alleged by the most plausible apologists of Hinduism that, although educated men can dispense with the idol and yet be religious, the common uneducated people cannot ; and hence it would neither be safe nor wise to withdraw from them this support of their lower spiritual life. Thus do these advocates of idolatry find a prudential and even a psychological justification for their religious expediency. Or, as it was once strikingly put by Sir Radha Kanta Deb, by far the greatest representative of the Sobha Bazaar family—" As you Europeans give *dolls* to *your* children, so do we Hindoos give these *idols* to *our* children, to our uneducated women and common people, who cannot do without them, but"—adding with an expressive smile—" we do not really worship them ourselves." This conscious yielding of such leaders to idolatry is, then, at the best, but a kindly *accommodation* to the popular prejudice and ignorance, and is even ultimately grounded upon the supposed *necessity* of their intellectual limitations.

Now, without denying that there *is* a great principle of charitable accommodation to the exigencies of the religious life in all circumstances, and without discussing, in the meantime, the range of its proper objects, I do most emphatically assert that this is *not* a legitimate application of it. To every earnest mind it must be evident, to begin with, that in the religious sphere every form of accommodation must be essentially pure and ultimately defensible. A doll is in every respect a proper object for a child, so long as he or she speaks as a child, understands as a child, and thinks as a child ; but this cannot be said of the objects of the Hindu idolatry. No delicate mind can look into a Shiva temple without a shudder. The horrid and bloody Kali, with her protruding tongue, her necklace of skulls, and her girdle of giant hands, is fitted only to excite terror and despair. The elephant-headed, huge-paunched Ganapati may excite the ridicule even of children, but can never draw forth their love. And to take the special example in point of the Krishna cult, what is it at the best, with all its merry music and mincing movements, but the apotheosis of sensual desire and the idolatry of merely finite life ? The preliminary and indispensable condition of childlike simplicity and moral pureness does *not* therefore apply to the popular Hinduism ; but the reverse. We never, in the highest light of reason, need become ashamed of our dolls or playthings ; but may even treasure them up to our latest hours as relics of our most innocent affections and of our purest joys. The idol, on the contrary, can only become to the maturer thought of its votaries, the symbol of the most unhallowed associations and of the earliest defilement of the soul.

But the fundamental position of the defender of idolatry is, that it is *an intellectual necessity* for the practical devotion of less cultivated minds. The essential nature of Deity is held to be so abstract and transcendent, that the ordinary worshipper cannot apprehend it intellectually, and hence he must have put before him some visible representation of the Divine. This is the sheet-anchor of the Hindu apologist to which he binds the whole system ; but it will not stand the slightest trial or strain. If this were true of the Hindu mind, nothing more degrading or humiliating could be said of it by its greatest despisers ; for it would thus be shewn to be by inherent nature and not merely by accidental degeneracy, much lower than that of the lowest races and tribes. If the Christian Missions have done nothing else, they have at least established the universal spirituality of human nature, by the practical demonstration of raising even the most debased savages in a single generation from the grossest idolatry up to the purest worship of God as "a Spirit, in spirit and in truth." And to take examples nearer at hand and on a somewhat higher stage of intellectual life, shall it be said that the high-born idealistic Bengali is of a lower order of intelligence than the Karen and the Kol, the Santhal and the Lepcha ? We know how etherial and incorporeal were the original abstractions of the Brahmanic doctrine, and the Hindus may even appropriate the boast of the Greeks and of the Germans, that they are a people of born philosophers. The history of Hinduism itself is the most evident refutation of its own aberrations and corruptions. Even in the present day, there is probably not a votary of the traditional idolatry but dimly feels the falsity of this defence of his practice, in the frequent sense of a permanent and independent Something higher than his idol. And if objection be taken to Christian examples, although they are the most relevant of all, the fifty millions of Mohammedans in India, who have so largely preserved the intellectual austerity of their great founder, most overwhelmingly show that no idol is required even here for the most devout and concentrated worship of the Divine Personality. Let it not then be said that the Hindu is by inner nature so coarse and low, that he cannot think of God without the aid of an image manufactured by his own hands!

If these historical examples, including, as they do, the whole past history of Christendom, are thought insufficient to overthrow the philosophical theory of idolatry, I am prepared to follow the Apologist into any labyrinthine depths of psychological analysis, and to show its fundamental groundlessness in view of the constitution and activities of the human mind. It cannot be denied that a supersensuous Reason is the most essential characteristic of human intelligence, for all philosophy, Asiatic or European, begins with it as its central principle and problem. And yet, what is idolatry but a practical treason against this royal crown of our manhood, and the setting up of the sensuous Imagination, even within the Holy of holies, in its stead? As all our spiritual dignity consists of thought or arises out of thought, the most melancholy suicide of all is that which extinguishes the light and life of the divine Reason within, and leaves the mere animated organism the sport of chemical change and decay. It would be out of place to enter here upon the subtle discussions that are still being carried on in the schools of philosophy, as to the range and limit of this inner spiritual faculty: it is enough to take our stand upon the fact that its existence is more or less admitted by all, and is asserted with no greater emphasis than in the Hindu systems. If, then, any vision of God, as the Being who transcends all sense, be possible in any degree to man, it must be attained through the inner and not through the outer eye; and according to a natural law, the more faithfully "the vision and the faculty divine" is exercised, the clearer will the views of its object become, and the more unworthy must all outward representations of the Infinite and the Eternal begin to appear. And let it not be said that this is only possible to philosophers, or to the gifted sons of poetic thought. Even the youngest and frailest child has it in germ. There is no principle more certain in mental science than this, that all the faculties belong to all men, however different may be their degree of exercise or power. Even such a plain, common-place thinker as

Dr Reid could see in the lowest savage all the seeds of the philosopher, the orator, the moralist, and the saint; and a thousand higher names might be cited from all the annals of philosophy in support of the same great truth. However we may ultimately settle the very difficult question as to the essential limits of religious thought, it is evident to all that Thought, and not sense, must eventually be recognised as the true organ of religion. And without entering on the perplexing problems of the relation of the finite to the Infinite, and of the temporal to the Eternal in the highest processes of thought, it is equally certain that the Infinite and the Eternal, however they are to be apprehended, cannot possibly be represented in finite form by even the most perfect efforts of human art. If all the vastness and wonder of the finite universe cannot satisfy the human yearning after a spiritual conception of God, how shall a paltry image made by an unspiritual workman ever shew forth more clearly or fully His Eternal Power and Godhead? And if the images of the idolator are *unnecessary* according to the essential constitution of the soul, and in presence of the divine panorama of the universe, why should even the simplest of our kind be further deluded for an hour into believing otherwise, when we can by a single kindly word awaken them out of their foolish dream?

But I go even further than this, and confidently affirm that all true psychology shows the utter irrationality and the impotence of any form of idolatry, for all the proper purposes of the religious life. If ever man could construct a material image of God, it would only be possible if He showed the pattern of Himself on the highest mount of inspiration. But the Hindoo idolmaker has had no such vision, and does not even claim to have had it. Hence he can only draw the forms of his imagery out of himself; and his images can only at the best represent his own subjective moods of feeling or aspiration, and not the known, transcendent, divine reality. The idol is but an external reflection of the spiritual life of the idolator. As Xenophanes, a great Greek thinker, said, the idolator makes his god in his own image. He gives his feeling visible objectivity in it, and it is but himself he sees in his idol and worships as his god. Strangest illusion of all,—the image-worshipper cowering in terror or flinging himself in a wild extasy of excitement before this dead obverted image of himself! What is Krishna, after all, but an imaginary embodiment of the sensuous feeling of the East, by an exaggeration of a mythological fancy to the supposed dimensions of the Divine?

But by a law of reason, the illusion cannot last, and terrible is the hour of awaking from this world of shadows. The first touch of the rising sun of knowledge dispels the nightmare of the dreamers, and forthwith the illusion vanishes, never to be recalled. And these learned men who stood in apparent reverence before the image of *Gopinathjee* at the great *shradh*, knew it well, and must have felt with inward bitterness that the faith of their youth had fled, and that they were standing there before the last sham of the nineteenth century in Bengal. Their fate is a hard one ; and will grow harder henceforth every day, if they do not yet put away their idols and feel after the living God. Mere intellectual enlightenment, wedded to idolatry, has here, as everywhere else, begotten its natural progeny of Agnosticism and Atheism and utter Scepticism. The new insight that has seen into the mere materialism and deadness of the old idol, has led by a natural reaction to a universal despair of the Divine. And so the idols remain as the playthings of the idlesse of later years, or at most as the lifeless symbols or names of *an unknown God* ; and the devout worship of them by the unsophisticated crowd, is but occasionally patronised at a splendid ceremonial, with a condescending smile.

Methinks, if the great Apostle of the Gentiles, in his burning love of fallen humanity and his unwearied proclamation of divinest truth, had appeared in the palatial Rajbaree compound on Sunday morning last, his irresistible earnestness would have stilled the stir and tumult of the idolatrous crowd for an hour, and he would have poured forth again the oration which he delivered among kindred surroundings of Stoics and Epicureans and mere curious idlers in the metropolis of Greek wisdom and art, and said :

YE MEN OF CALCUTTA, "I perceive that in all things ye are too superstitious. For as I passed by, and beheld your devotions, I found an altar with this inscription, TO THE UNKNOWN GOD. Whom therefore ye ignorantly worship, Him declare I unto you. God that made the world and all things therein, seeing that he is Lord of heaven and earth, dwelleth not in temples made with hands; neither is worshipped with men's hands as though He needed anything, seeing He giveth to all life, and breath, and all things; And hath made of one blood all nations of men for to dwell on all the face of the earth, and hath determined the times before appointed, and the bounds of their habitation, that they should seek the Lord if haply they might feel after Him and find Him, though He be not far from any one of us. For in Him we live and move and have our being; as certain also of your own poets have said 'For we are also his offspring.' *Forasmuch then as we are the offspring of God, we ought not to think that the Godhead is like unto gold, or silver, or stone graven by art and man's device.*"

If the learned men who on Sunday last yielded a homage unworthy of themselves to the degrading idolatry of their forefathers, will not listen to any poor words of mine, I fervently beseech them at least to meditate with open heart and soul, as they well can, upon these glorious utterances of the great Apostle of the Gentiles who bore the whole world of the idolatrous children of God so tenderly upon his heart. Every word of them might indeed have been spoken yesterday here in this Calcutta, and been written down for the first time to-day; and yet though eighteen centuries old, the world has not exhausted their length of human comprehensiveness, their breadth of affectionate charity, or their depth of philosophic wisdom. May these most interesting searchers after truth around us, like the wisest of the children of men since that unparalleled oration was delivered to the Athenians on Mars Hill, also find *their* Divine light and guidance out of all the darkness and sorrows of time through this same Paul of the ancient Minor Asia, who was Divinely called to his office even for their sakes too, and whom the ages since have shewn to be the greatest of all the followers of JESUS CHRIST.

W. HASTIE.

The General Assembly's Institution,
September 22, 1882.

## III.

### THE ALLEGED HARMLESSNESS OF IDOLATRY.

### To the Editor.

Sir,—It is most interesting, not only historically but practically within these similar surroundings, to ponder with earnest care the way in which Paul of Tarsus, the most philosophical and the most eloquent of Christians, refuted the idolatry of the ancient Athenians. His method is very instructive, and cannot be too diligently considered by Pagan apologist, or Christian missionary. He evidently adopted the only line of argument that would be pronounced logical in *any* case,—the only one, therefore, which could be wisely employed with the skilled dialecticians of the Grecian schools. He refuted their idolatry on rational grounds, by appealing from the lower sensuous feelings of their common mind to that higher light of Reason which still witnesses to Eternal truth in all men, however it may be "shorn of its beams" or outwardly obscured. Paul addressed the men of Athens as "too superstitious," or as very much given to the idolatrous worship of Gods. He had seemed to them a "setter forth of strange gods, because he preached unto them Jesus and the Resurrection"; but his very first words, which are graceful and tender rather than harsh and severe, indicate that he is not about to plunge them into a new form of superstitious belief, but to emancipate them from their superstition entirely. Their idolatry was false, he argued first of all, because it was *essentially unworthy of God.* The one God of this great universe is not to be worshipped by the products of man's hands, nor to be represented by them ; for He is infinite and absolute and all-sufficient in Himself, so that as the heaven of heavens cannot contain Him, He needeth not human temples for his residence, nor the art-forms of his own creatures for His pleasure. The Divine Majesty *cannot* be figured to human eyes nor embodied by human hands. " We *ought not* to think that the Godhead is like unto gold, or silver, or stone graven by art or man's device."—And he further refutes the Athenian idolatry, by appealing to *its own manifest acknowledgement of failure.* All this elaborate ceremonialism and ritual had only hidden the One God from the souls of men, instead of bringing Him nearer to them ; and it ends with a public confession of total ignorance concerning the true being and character of God as *the Unknown.* With this same melancholy acknowledgment does all mere Pagan religion end. So, for instance, had it been with the mysterious religion of ancient Egypt. Plutarch tells us of a temple of Isis, in that ancient home of wisdom and art, over whose portal was inscribed those deeply suggestive words : " I AM ALL THAT WAS AND IS AND SHALL BE, *but no one of mortals has lifted my veil.*" Exactly thus did Paul find it at Athens, " the eye of Greece, mother of arts and eloquence." The wisdom of the cultivated and thoughtful Greeks had ended after centuries of the most patient and enquiring investigation, in dedicating a prominent altar to "the Unknown God." What bright light and life going out in darkness and death!

But Paul, having shown the irrationality of the national idolatry, does not end with the mere inanity of a religious negation; he only purges the minds of his hearers of their superstitious fancies that he may carry them up into the pure light of the higher revealed knowledge of God. "Whom, therefore, ye ignorantly worship, Him declare I unto you." 'Ye worship, and so far ye do well; but ye worship ye know not what; and I have come to declare to you the true nature and character of the Being ye ought to worship, and thus to substitute for your false and idolatrous imaginations, the true conception of God which ye are all capable of appropriating.' The conception of God unfolded by Paul involves two simple elements which yet contain the sum of all theology; (1) God *the universal Creator*, the Lord of heaven and earth, the one Almighty God, the Maker and Upholder of all finite things, including man; (2) God *the Universal Father of all spirits*, whose "offspring" even these idolatrous Athenians were, as one of their own poets called Aratus had well said, and, as the Pantheistic Stoics were wont to say "in Whom we live and move and have our being." Now both these elements in Paul's conception of God had been received by him through Divine Revelation; the former from the historical records of the Old Testament, the latter by the inward illumination of a life "hid with Christ in God." The first verse of Genesis sounds the keynote of all religious truth; "in the beginning God created the heavens and the earth." Yet the highest thought of Greece, even her loftiest philosophy—the philosophy of Plato—had not attained it, for even to his ideal spirit the external was eternal, and matter was unmade. The doctrine of the Divine Fatherhood—a higher truth in itself—had, however, been vaguely seen by their thinkers and poets, who vitalised and even humanized all the processes of nature; but in the popular religion the great truth was degraded and defiled and even brutified. Yet note how delicately and tenderly their very defective apprehension of it, is dealt with. It is the highest thought of God,—there is no truth beyond it even in Christianity; it is the most inward relation of God, for He cannot be brought closer than in His fatherly love to the human heart. Yet Paul does not speak of it to the Athenians as if it were a great esoteric secret, or a new and unfathomable mystery which he alone had apprehended. On the contrary, he appeals to one of their most obscure poets, who had lived 300 years before, to prove that it was not a mere Jewish myth, but was explicitly contained in the workings and aspirations of the Aryan mind. The Athenians only required to have its highest moral meaning unfolded to them, and to recognise its Divinest exhibition in history, to be recalled from their idolatrous errors and to have all their yearnings and longings after God—their seeking and feeling after Him, brought to satisfaction and rest. For this "Unknown God," the Almighty Maker of heaven and earth, this Eternal "Father of all," though He dwelleth not in temples made with hands, is " not far from any one of us," and had even entered into human life and become as one of the sons of men.

All this applies most literally to the Hindu idolatry; and only on that account has it been introduced here. And the well-known reason is that the Hindu and the Greek idolatry were twin branches on the same original Aryan stem, and all knowledge of the one is knowledge of the other also. The discoveries of comparative philology and theology have proved this beyond all question long since; and now the comparative method is only working out the relation more fully in detail. The most striking thing that the classical student of Greece and Rome finds in India, is not its brighter star-jewels sparkling on the brow of night, nor its sunny groves of palm by day, nor even the graceful forms of its flowing-robed men moving in the dusky dawn, but the visible exhibition around him of his early dreams of the old classical world. With his own eyes he sees the Jupiter and Juno, the Apollo and Minerva, the Mars and Venus of Homer and Virgil again. All the greater gods of Olympus seem still " to rule the middle air," in exaggerated form; the minor divinities in more countless crowds still haunt every meadow, grove and stream of the further East; and dreamy devotees still wear the symbols of their gods and throng the ancient fanes and shrines. Let it not be said that our European scholars do not understand Hinduism. It is they who have seen all its mysteries first, in the clear modern daylight of contrasting light and shade ; and who have explained its every enigma to its puzzled and petrified priests. And all that Paul proved so truly of the brighter and fairer Hellenism, applies most literally to the darker and gloomier Hinduism, the last tenacious survival of the old Aryan world, and the strangest religious anachronism of the modern age.

All idolatry, then, Hindu or Greek, is essentially and even blasphemously unworthy of God, and is of no avail as a help to the genuine aims of the religious life. But even if it be conceded that idolatry is not only intellectually indefensible, whatever ingenuity of metaphor may be called in to its aid, and if it further be admitted to be spiritually useless and only misleading : it may still be maintained—and is indeed commonly maintained—that after all *it is morally harmless* and may well be let alone. This childish playing at gods and goddesses, it is alleged, is but the spiritual amusement of uneducated minds, and manlier natures may quietly let it pass as only a harmless play of redundant life. It quickens the mental life of the children ; it lights up the dungeon gloom of the zenana with an occasional ray ; it feeds the hungry where nothing else will, and even calls forth phantom laughter amid the stifling atmosphere of death. And so we have but too many advocates even among careless English onlookers of the so-called harmlessness of idolatry, for no other reason than its apparent merriment, and because in presence of it, their own hard, heartless, weary world still holds on.

But again, at the very outset, it seems too evidently irrational and unreal even to suppose, that the loss or want of the knowledge of the One True God could ever be harmless or insignificant at any stage of man's history. If the whole universe and all the ongoings of human life are grounded ultimately upon His eternal Will and Purpose, how *can* they possibly be a matter of indifference to the habit of our action even in the present world? In the earlier stages of intellectual development especially, not to know God is not to know duty; and without duty, life becomes void of any intelligent object or law. And although this may be concealed beneath unreflecting custom for a time, so that the external arrangements of society–such as the caste laws–may mechanically uphold a moral order, yet the growth of intelligence will in time throw off all such restraints and lead to unbridled licentiousness, unless the individual from the indwelling consiousness of the Divine has already become a Law to himself. The question of the possibility of an independent obligatory morality need not be raised here, for the idolator, as such, moves on a stage of life where the idea is, as yet, entirely unknown. His worship is his only representative of spiritual obligation; and if it be a false worship, he has nothing but mere sensuous impulse left upon which to build the structure of his life. It cannot, therefore, be a matter of moral indifference whether he is an idolator or no; but on the contrary, his idolatry will determine the whole substance and complexion of his morality.

Looked at in this line still more closely, all the forms of polytheistic idolatry are really ignorant of Divine law, which can only have its ultimate origin in the Divine Personality, and they are therefore *not morally entitled to be regarded as religions at all,* since they want that element of Divine obligation which is the root principle of all true religion. David Hume, in his keen subtle way, has most clearly seen this, and most strikingly expressed it. " To any one who considers justly of the matter," he says, " it will appear that the gods of the polytheists are no better than the elves and fairies of our ancestors, and merit as little as any pious worship and veneration. These pretended religionists *are really a kind of superstitious atheists,* and acknowledge no being that corresponds to our idea of a Deity. No first principle of mind or thought; no supreme government and administration; no Divine contrivance or intention in the fabric of the world." And so it really is, polytheistic Idolatry is but another name for a superstitious Atheism, because it does not grasp the real being and character of the only True God. The extremes of a bounded Atheism and of a boundless Polytheism meet. No god and 33 crores of gods amount objectively to the same thing as regards God, and the Atheist has the advantage of having got rid of his superstition, which is all that is peculiar to the Polytheist. And as Bacon has well shown in his celebrated Essay, an immoral Superstition is worse than a pure Atheism, for " it were better to have no opinion of God at all than such an opinion as is unworthy of Him; the one is unbelief, the other is contumely, and certainly, superstition is the reproach of the Deity." This being so, we at once see the utter illusiveness and the demoralising unreality of idolatry. There is really NO GOD anywhere in the universe who will own to be *Kali*, or *Karttik* or *Krishna*, or *Shiva*, or *Durga*, or *Ganesh*, or *Hanuman*, however the poor votaries may be pityingly excused or mercifully forgiven. The idolator but babbles to the wind and plays with the echo of his own names. A philosophical analysis thus resolves the whole 330 millions of Gods in the Hindu Pantheon into mere subjective spectres. They "are such stuff as dreams are made of" and the Bengali idolator, like Ixion of old, still embraces but a cloud when he stretches out his hands to his divinity.

And when to this essential emptiness of the idolatrous worship, we conjoin the inner distraction which necessarily arises out of the endless multiplicity of its objects, it is most evident that the Hindu idolator can find in the indefinite chaos of his antagonistic, inconsistent, and contradictory gods no sure, satisfying type of the spiritual life. Each of them, besides, when taken apart as an example, is full of finite frailty,—mutable, fickle, partial, capricious, uncertain, "every thing by turns and nothing long." Polytheism sheds no intellectual light on the order of the universe, and it furnishes no pole-stars of guidance beyond merest impulse and chance over the billows of time. Hence even viewed theoretically, the whole system must vanish again among the shadows of "chaos and old night," before the certain all-conquering discovery by modern science of the unity of the universe and the harmony of all its parts.

And when, above all, we take into account the *character* of these innumerable divinities and their assimilative influence upon their votaries, the proof against *the alleged harmlessness of the Hindu idolatry* becomes too sadly overwhelming. Hinduism with all its apparent humanity is but a disguised Nature-worship like the Vedic ceremonialism from which it ultimately sprang; and it is in consequence pervaded all through by the mere animal licentiousness of the natural man. Notwithstanding all that has been written about the myriotheistic idolatry of India, no pen has yet adequately depicted all the hideousness and grossness of the monstrous system. It has been well described by one who knew it, as "Satan's masterpiece of ingenuity for the entanglement of souls," and as "the most stupendous fortress and citadel of ancient error and idolatry now in the world. Its foundations pierce downwards into the Stygian pool; its walls and battlements, crusted over with the hoar of untold centuries, start upwards into the clouds. It is defended by 330 millions of gods and goddesses, —the personations of evil, of types and forms to be parallelled only by the spirits of Pandemonium. Within are congregated a hundred and fifty millions of human captives, the willing victims of the most egregious 'falsities and lies' that have ever been hatched by the Prince of Darkness,—pantheisms and atheisms, rationalisms and legends, and all-devouring credulities, with fastings and ablutions, senseless mummeries, loathsome impurities, and bloody barbarous sacrifices, in number and variety vastly surpassing all that is to be found in the world besides." No Western poet, in his wildest dream, ever imagined such a "Den of error," or planted such monsters by the gates of Hell. The moral pollutions of the system cannot be decently referred to on the page of a modern newspaper. If we take the boasted literature of the so-called *holy Shastras*, in which the system is mirrored, every pure mind must turn away from it in loathing and disgust. The immoralities of the Western idolatry from Homer and Hesiod and Aristophanes and Lucian, to Ovid and Juvenal and Petronius Arbiter, are here a thousand times outdone. With much that was noble and healthy in its early stages, the Sanskrit literature, became infected by a moral leprosy which gradually spread like a corrupting disease through almost all its fibres and organs. The great Sanskrit scholars of Bengal know too well what I mean, and dare not say a word in defence of this later literature, nor even translate it into modern tongues. The hideous fancies of the Linga Purana and its associates, and the putrid mass of the Tantras are the most melancholy inheritance of Young India from the past. Only to think that this has been the principal pabulum of the spiritual life of the Hindus for about a thousand years, and the loudly boasted lore of their semi-deified priests! Need we seek elsewhere for the foul disease that has been preying upon the vitals of the national life, and reducing the people to what they are? "Shew me your gods," cried an ancient Greek apologist, "and I will shew you your men." The Hindu is just what his idol gods have made him. His own idolatry, and not foreign conquerors, has been the curse of his history. No people was ever degraded except by itself, and this is most literally so with the Hindu. As we trace the progress of the national idolatry from stage to stage, we see "Religion blushing, veil her sacred fire, and unawares Morality expire." And along with them went public spirit and private virtue, until the ancient Bharata became the easy prey of every non-idolatrous adventurer in turn. And so the heroic ages passed away, with their simple faith, their brave leaders, their virtuous ladies, and their melodious bards; and this debasing idolatry produced, according, to the painful testimony of native writers themselves, a mass of shrinking cowards, of unscrupulous deceivers, of bestial idlers, of filthy songsters, of degraded women, and of lustful men. God forbid that I should charge any of these things upon the cultivated gentlemen who took part in the great *shradh*; on the contrary, I sincerely believe they have all emancipated themselves from the blight of these influences, and in that is my hope. But I do charge publicly upon them the guilt of a thoughtless external acquiescence in the form of the system, and under whatever euphemism or metaphor or euhemerism, they may themselves take refuge, the untutored worshipper of Krishna and Durga has none, so that the chains of this accursed Belial are but rivetted by such examples more firmly upon his soul, whereas a word from them would at once break all his shackles, and enable him to rise into even a higher spiritual light and liberty than their own.

So far then from the Hindu idolatry being harmless, it has ever been, and in these progressive days of light, it still is, the one chief cause of all the demoralisation and degradation of India. It has consecrated and encouraged every conceivable form of licentiousness, falsehood, injustice, cruelty, robbery, murder. It has taught the millions every possible iniquity by the example of their gods, but has not even given them a name for the sense of moral obligation in their speech. Its sublimest spiritual states have been but the reflex of physiological conditions in disease. It has dissipated the highest intellectual capacity in the muttering of senseless incantations. Every Hindu home is still polluted with idols, and the opening senses meet their abominations at every turn. The children drink in the hideous spirit of demons with their mother's milk, and cannot learn to speak without the foulest words. Rational men wear the sign of beastly gods unabashed upon their foreheads, and have lost the modesty of manhood. The Hindu alone still disgraces the nobility of the Aryan race by a Syrian worship of idols, inflaming him with lust, under every green tree.

O Bharata-Varsha, the once fair daughter of the

Morning, how hast thou fallen from thy throne of pride and become the mother of harlots and of the abominations of the earth! Well might the Lord God say of thee, as He once did of ancient Israel, "Thou hast defiled thyself in thine idols which thou hast made; therefore, have I made thee a reproach unto the heathen and a mocking to all countries."

If it be fancied that in all this there is any accent of exaggeration, then let us turn from the uncertain opinions of prejudiced men to the severe veracity of the Apostle, and hear how he traces the progress of idolatry even in the noblest spirits of the ancient world from the clear primal knowledge of God, through the voluntary darkening of the inward light and the perverted caricaturing of the Divine glory, till all the abominations of sin and shame are brought forth in the myriad monstrous forms of superstitious night.

"That which may be known of God is manifest in them; for God hath shewed it unto them. For the invisible things of Him are clearly seen being understood by the things that are made even His Eternal Power and God-head; so *that they are without excuse;* because that when they knew God, they glorified Him not as God, neither were thankful; but became vain in their imaginations and their foolish hearts were hardened. Professing themselves to be wise they became fools, and changed the glory of the uncorruptible God into an image made like to corruptible man, and to birds and four-footed beasts and creeping things. Wherefore God also gave them up to uncleanness through the lusts of their own hearts, to dishonour their own bodies between themselves; who changed the truth of God into a lie, and worshipped and served the creature more than the Creator, Who is blessed for ever. Amen. For this cause God gave them up unto vile affection. . . And even as they did not like to retain God in their knowledge, God gave them over to a reprobate mind to do those things which are not convenient ; being filled with all unrighteousness, fornication, wickedness, covetousness, maliciousness ; full of envy, murder, debate, deceit, malignity ; whisperers, backbiters, haters of God ; despiteful, proud, boasters, inventors of evil things, disobedient to parents ; without understanding, covenant-breakers, without natural affection, implacable, unmerciful ; who, knowing the judgment of God, that they which commit such things are worthy of death, not only do the same but have pleasure in them that do them."—( ROMANS : I, 19-32. )

Alas ! that such a description of humanity should ever have been written by the purest of men, and still more that it should have been so true.

I put it to Hindu scholars whether this Paul, reared in its midst and with the awful spectacle of its worst corruptions before his eyes, did not understand idolatry in all its movements and issues, and whether they were not merely "the words of truth and soberness" when he wrote that " the wrath of God is revealed from heaven against all ungodliness and unrighteousness of men who hold the truth in unrighteousness" ? I further put it to them whether these issues of the " reprobate mind " have not been brought forth, and are being brought forth, as abundantly and as loathsomely here by the Hindu idolatry, as they were by the twin sister of Greece ; and whether this has not been the real cause of all the social evils of India ? And I beseech them in consequence, again, to listen to the inspired orator of Mars Hill as he brings his philosophical exposure of the futility and degradation of idolatry to a close, with his earnest exposition of the Divine purpose and consummation of the world's history. 'God is the Creator of the world and the Father of the spirits of all men; but He is more. He is *the moral Governor of the human race.*' His government is "patient because He is eternal," but it is sure and must overcome in the end. "And the times of this ignorance God has winked at,"—in other words, God has given scope to the natural will of man in the past, and out of his long-suffering He tolerates its working still. But men have *not* acknowledged the the Father-God alone, and He will not be finally mocked by His own children. He alone has given them life and breath and all things; but they have not rendered Him the undivided worship of their pure love and gratitude in return. They have practically disowned His Fatherhood, whatever fine things the poets may have said of it; they have introduced division and discord and death into the human family, and have even denied its equal origin from Him. They have put the creature in place of the Creator; themselves and their handiwork in place of their God. And if God has been patient, it has been because He would graciously lead men to *repentance*. Longer will He not overlook this human travesty of Himself, or endure this wilful violation of His order and law, but now—even "*now commandeth all men everywhere to repent.*" And the reason and proof of this commandment are the impending day of the final righteous judgment of men and the awful appearing of the Christ, once the suffering Lamb of God, but then the inexorable Judge of all. "Because He hath appointed a day in which He will judge the world in righteousness, by that man whom He hath ordained; *whereof He hath given assurance unto all men*" (for rational man could not accept it without assurance, and Paul had received the assured proof of an ocular demonstration) "IN THAT HE HATH RAISED HIM FROM THE DEAD."

Before the combined terror of the world to come and the safety of the Divine Resurrection let us pause; and as Paul once wrote to the converts he loved above all others at the close of his solemn exhortations, let me also be allowed to say with all friendly earnestness to my Hindu readers: "THINK ON THESE THINGS."

W. HASTIE.

The General Assembly's Institution,
September 24, 1882.

---

# IV.

## THE ULTIMATE PHILOSOPHY OF BRAHMANISM.

### To the Editor.

Sir,—Many of the educated Hindus, when it is earnestly put to them, are willing to admit the undeniable evils of the popular Idolatry. They even pity the benighted people, and sometimes cherish a faint hope that the *patshala* may yet raise them to their own high level of approach towards that ultimate emancipation from the flesh, which has been, for so many centuries, the weird dream of the Hindu devotee. The speculative gymnosophist will even repudiate the popular idolatry as a sensuous delusion ; he claims an esoteric wisdom which raises himself far above it ; and if its noisy turmoil breaks in upon his calm serenity of soul, he only withdraws the farther from its transitory stir, in order to sink the deeper in dreamy indolence into the unfathomable depths of Brahm. In the spiritual warfare against Hinduism, it is, therefore, not enough to storm the outworks of the popular idolatry ; its defenders must be followed up into their last retreat, in *the great metaphysical abstraction*, which they believe to be the impregnable inner citadel of the whole system. Here, indeed, we have to encounter an entirely opposite form of life and thought, as different from the vulgar sensuousness, as is the cold lifeless silence of the pole from the warm exuberant naturalism of the tropics. Hinduism is, indeed, the most comprehensive, because the most contradictory, of systems. If " variety is the life of nature, " we have it here ; but where is the unity that is to reduce the variety to harmony ? These elect souls, so far removed in their metaphysical sublimity from " the madding crowd's ignoble strife," seem indeed to belong, as they themselves claim, to a higher race ; and like certain spirits described by Milton, can only feed apart on the sweeter eloquence of the soul :

> " Others apart sat on a hill retired,
> In thoughts more elevate and reasoned high
> Of Providence, Foreknowledge, Will and Fate,
> Fixed fate, free will, foreknowledge absolute.
> Of good and evil much they argued then,
> Of happiness and final misery,
> Passion, and apathy, and glory, and shame.

These are none other than the venerable surviving Rishis of Bharata-Varsha,—" Those grey spirits yearning in desire To follow knowledge, like a sinking star, Beyond the utmost bound of human thought." And with them are their more mundane pupils, the scholars of modern India, who have assiduously imbibed their ancient lore, and mingled with it the latest superficialities of Western thought. These mighty-minded " Lords of those who know," seated on the highest pinnacle of thought, condescend betimes, like the Olympians of old, to look over " the crystal battlements " and down upon the ongoings of vulgar life in the sweltering plains ; but their hearts know neither passion, nor hope, nor care. When their dreamy eyes catch the spectacle of white-faced men from the far

West, in earnest expostulation with the idolatrous crowd,—they but faintly smile. The cry of passionate appeal for aid in the struggle to save dying men, rises to their ears, but they only yawn, being afraid even to nod assent, like Olympian Jove, lest they might shake the spheres. In serene self-complacency they even scorn the missionary as well as the crowd; and in a "Divine oblivion of low-thoughted care," dream the century's opportunity away. Not for them the burden of daily toil, nor the strenuous duty of change. All is well, whispers the sentinel, in the vast of space; and the Divine only dwells in the ether of the inane!

> " In the hollow Lotus-land they live and lie reclined
> On the hills, like Gods together, careless of mankind.
> For they lie beside their nectar and the bolts are hurled
> Far below them in the valleys, and the clouds are lightly curl'd
> Round their golden houses, girdled with the gleaming world:
> Where they smile in secret, looking over wasted lands,
> Blight and famine, plague and earthquake, roaring deeps and fiery sands,
> Clanging fights and flaming towns, sinking ships and praying hands,
> *But they smile*, they find a music centred in a doleful song
> Steaming up, a lamentation and an ancient tale of wrong,
> Like a tale of little meaning, though the words are strong;
> Chanted from an ill-used race of men that cleave the soil,
> Sow the seed and reap the harvest with enduring toil,
> Storing yearly little dues of wheat and rice and oil;
> Till they perish and they suffer,—some, 'ts whisper'd, down in hell

> Suffer endless anguish, others in Elysian valleys dwell,
> Resting weary limbs at last on beds of asphodel."

Yea, we all know it, "Surely, surely, slumber is more sweet than toil." But alas! the sweet complacency and ease of this slumberous idealism can no longer avail. All its pretentiousness and security are gone. The crystal battlements have been scaled by the daring scholars of the West, and their keen eyes have searched through every nook and corner of the beatific abode. And with however feeble steps, and at however great an interval, I shall venture to follow their bold and safe guidance up the giant heights, and even dare for a moment to look steadily into the placid faces of the "twice-born" Himalayans. And once fairly upon this highest and last retreat of the speculative Rishi, it will not be so dificult to shew, as at first sight appears, that his metaphysical system cannot answer even one of the great questions of our modern world, and that the whole of the Brahmanic theology never really solved a single problem of human life or thought.

Here, indeed, it would be out of place to range over these fundamental questions in detail,—or to discuss them with the special technicalities of the schools; but it may be possible to touch them at least with the finger of a living interest, and remembering in dealing with the wise, the adage *verbum sat sapienti*—a mere indication of argument may suffice.

It is now an old truism to say, that the ultimate

principle of the Brahmanic doctrine is Pantheism; but it is not so evident that it is a Pantheism which, instead of supporting, immediately subverts the reality of the finite world. Taking one lofty bound out of the sphere of sense and all its perplexing entanglements, the Brahman thinker ascends at once to the "supersensuous reason," from which serene altitude he resolves the finite world into Nothing, as a mere *Maya* or dreamlike illusion of sense, and finds the one and sole reality of the universe in the infinite and eternal Thought which he calls *Brahm*. Brahmanism is thus the extremest form of negative Idealism that can be conceived; and we can only approach it by a persistent and uncompromising denial of all the reality we have ever experienced. In its negation of the world of sense, it goes far beyond Plato or Spinoza or Berkeley or Hume. Yet this is the one central principle of all the orthodox Hindu authorities, including the Vedas, the Upanishads, the Vedanta system of philosophy, and the great commentator Sankaracharya, the reviver of Brahmanism after the Buddhist ascendancy and the ablest expounder of its creed. This Brahm is the god of the emancipated Brahman, and to him more truly may be attributed what Scheleiermacher said so strikingly of Spinoza, that "intellectually intoxicated by the infinite god, he reduces the world to a mere allegory, and finds in it only a non-existent shadow-form of his own conscious vacancy; the Infinite is his beginning and end, the universal his only and eternal love."

Perhaps the essence of the Brahmanical philosophy cannot be expressed more simply or more accurately than has been done by Monier Williams, and as he is a favourable and an unquestionable authority on the subject, his summary will give more authority and definiteness to the view :—

" A Vedantist's creed," he says, " has the merit of extreme simplicity, being comprised in the well known formula of three words from the Chandogya Upanishad (ekam evadvitiyam) 'one only essence without a second' [*i.e.* without any other] ; or in the following, 'Brahma exists truly, the world falsely, the soul is only Brahma, and no other' ; or in the following, 'All this universe, indeed, is Brahma ; from him does it proceed ; into him it is dissolved ; in him it breathes. So let every one adore him calmly'. .. In the Vedanta there is really no material world at all, as distinct from the universal soul. Hence, the doctrine of this school is called *A-dvaita*, Non-dualism. The universe exists but merely as a form of the eternal Essence. . . From other portions of the aphorisms, it appears the one universal Essence, called Brahma, is to the external world what yarn is to cloth, what milk to curds, what earth to a jar, what gold to a bracelet. This Essence is both Creator and creation, actor and act. It is itself existence, knowledge and joy ; but at the same time without parts, unbounded by qualities, without action, without motion, having no consciousness such as is denoted by 'I' and 'thou,' apprehending no person or thing, nor apprehended by any, having neither beginning nor end, immutable, the only real entity. If this be true, the pure Being must be almost identical with pure Nothing, so that the two extremes of Buddhistic Nihilism and Vedantic Pantheism, far as they profess to be apart, appear in the end to meet.'

Here, then, we have the great esoteric mystery of Brahmanism at last open to view, and stripped of all its excrescent multiform shapes and modifications. It is upon this thin shadowy abstraction ultimately that the faith of the millions of India has rested for so many centuries; it is *this* which is supposed to furnish a rational justification of all her idolatry and to form the intellectual crown of the wisest of mankind. The vulgar cannot, indeed, rise to the great Brahmanic thought, and it would have once been death for them even to have tried. But it is the same Brahm which they unconsciously perceive through the forms of sense, as he plays in the phantom forms of an infinite flitting godhead before their eyes, just as they see the same light shining through all the grotesque pictures of their many-sided coloured lanterns by night. In their wondering, sensuous, noisy idolism, then, they may wisely be let alone.

It is perhaps not to be wondered at, that the early Sanskrit scholars of Europe should have been taken by surprise, and even been carried away by this overawing conception. And even yet, not a few of them of praiseworthy philological industry and acuteness, but of superficial metaphysical gift and training, insist on seeing incomparably more in it than there is, and spend their fluent rhetoric upon its ill-timed and ill-deserved praise. The modern European mind, having risen again to the high altitudes of Plato and the invigorating atmosphere of Aristotle, and having seen through all the tangled emanational confusions of Gnosticism, having communed fully with Spinoza and Kant, and traversed all the heights and breadths and depths of Fichte, Shelling and Hegel, and being sobered and steadied by the realities of recent science, might surely have now passed out of its first amaze ; and recognised all the emptiness and futility and unreality of the Brahmanical idea.

( 1 ) First of all, it is obvious to remark that this negative idealism gives no satisfactory explanation of the existent world and its stable order, and consequently gives no foundation for the practical activities of life, or the objective interest of modern science. The mere evasion of "*a form of Brahm*" gives no intelligible meaning to external phenomena, or to their peculiarity of being, but only reduces them to a contradictory and unreal and fruitless negation. The marvellous universe around us, whatever it may be, is too uniform and real to be resolved into the mere phantastic self-amusement of an impersonal entity; and the individuality of nature and of organic life everywhere protests against it at every turn. The modern mind with its intense passion for present reality, which is its most striking characteristic cannot therefore tolerate such a theory for an hour, and the whole of modern science, physical and historical, is its increasing practical, irresistible refutation.—Or, as Professor Williams puts it: "The Vedanta theory, if pushed to its ultimate consequences, must lead to the neglect of all activity, physical and intellectual, and of all self-culture. If everything be God, then He and you and I must be one. Why should any efforts be made for the advancement of self or for the good of others ?" In this lifeless faith, then, and not merely in external climatic influences, do we find the ultimate explanation of the historical dreaminess and inaction of the Hindu.

(2) Again, this theory evidently gives no moral meaning or purpose to human life. Its moral indifference to the ongoings of sense, is its immediate ethical consequence. These are really nothing but passing illusions, and do not disturb the soul of things. The Brahman may indulge in all the pollutions of the flesh, and yet leave his Divine consciousness unsoiled. Much more then may the common people give way, with excuse, to unlimited passion; for it is their very "nature too." Hence the immorality of the popular idolatry not only receives no check, but derives its most unhallowed excuse from the ultimate principle of the system. Duty, as a Divine, controlling law of life, is unknown; and Hinduism, too, with all its severe abstract thought, but too palpably illustrates the apophthegm of a late great statesman that "every form of natural religion issues at last in the *orgy*."

(3) Brahmanism, again, manifestly leaves its votary ultimately in the melancholy and despair of "having no hope, and being without God in the world." Such a Pantheism is really at one with Materialism and Atheism, as regards the ultimate destiny of the soul. The only purpose it can assign to life is to get rid of the illusion of personality, as well as the vice of passion, and then to faint away on the last highest point of abstract thought into *the impersonal Unknowable*, as a star fades in the morning light or as a drop of water is lost in the infinite ocean.

In this one sole Essence, if nowhere else, it is surely manifest that "Something and Nothing are one and the same." But this impersonal infinite is really *not God.* It has not one of His attributes, or activities, or relations. It is everything and yet nothing; it plays through the vast of space and yet is eternally quiescent; it neither knows nor wills; it is neither known nor served. Hence, the more logical thinkers of India, finding no stay or support for their thought and life in the empty Brahm, when left to themselves, have invariably wandered into Materialism, or Atheism, or utter Agnosticism. And the logical sum of the system may be given in the following graphic words of a German philosopher: "I know absolutely nothing of any existence, not even of my own. I myself know nothing and am nothing. All reality is converted into a marvellous dream, without a life to dream of and without a mind to dream,—into a dream made up only of a dream of itself... Perception is a dream; and thought is the dream of that dream."

( 4 ) Hence the final result of the Brahmanic theology, as Monier Williams has hinted, is the dogmatic Nihilism of Buddha, the most logical thinker of his race. Buddhism, by its marvellous self-denial and perseverance, won and held the spiritual rule of India for several hundred years; but the blowing out of all things in the Nirvana was too outspoken and unreal a creed even for the Hindu, and a sound practical instinct expelled it from India. But, unhappily, for the history of this great people, Christianity did not come then in the hour of India's greatest need, and there was nothing to put in the place of the Buddhistic despair, but the old hollow faith, with only a more sensuous ritual, a more rigid *regime*, a more pretentious priesthood, and a more powerful drag upon the wheels of advancing time. And this India appears to-day as the natural and logical product of it all, to those who can see into the real causes of events and the Providence which overrules the insanity of nations.

Let it not then be said that we missionaries are so entirely ignorant of what Brahmanism is ; or that we have come, without reason, to interfere with the hallowed destiny of a chosen people. If educated Brahmans try the task of re-creating their country upon their own old basis, they cannot but fail. They have now had time enough for the trial, and all their resources have been brought into play. Their every effort is self-condemned. The success of a popular reform, according to their very aim, could only issue in a conscious extinction. Such a result would be its own completest refutation. The deeper the system is explored, the more clearly is it seen that its fundamental abstractions can hold no movement of thought or change of life, but must be given up to perpetual spiritual sterility. The system is at the negative pole of metaphysical reflection, and at the farthest possible remove from positive truth. No power on earth shall ever possibly fill it with life again. Every pulse of modern life and every step of onward movement are away from it, never to return. And as I may yet endeavour to show, a truer and profounder philosophy is demonstrating the all-important fact, that it is only CHRISTIANITY, with its revelation of the Divine Personality in all the fulness of His self-existent thought and eternal purpose, that can rationally take the place of the falling Brahmanism, so as to reconcile the sons of India, in a pure and blessed life, to the universe around them and to themselves.

W. HASTIE.

The General Assembly's Institution.
September 27, 1882.

## V.

## THE SOCIAL CHANGES OF A CENTURY IN INDIA.

### To the Editor.

SIR,—If the late Dowager Maharanee of Sobha Bazaar, who lived to the remarkable age of ninety-nine years, had been educated in her youth like a European lady, what a wonderful book she might have written, and what strange stories about her countrymen she would have transmitted to posterity. These 99 years of her long and honoured life, stretching as they did from the decisive conquests of the English at the close of the century and the first breaking of the old order under Western influences, to the beginnings of mass education and local self-government to-day, embrace the greatest social changes that will ever be seen in India. All future movement and progress can hardly be anything else than a wider development, with incidental external modifications, of the forces which this native lady must have seen or at least *felt* coming into operation. When she drew life's first breath, Warren Hastings was still in Bengal and in the highest flush of his power, having burst with masterful genius through the web of rancorous intrigue that had been woven around him by his English rivals, and being still all unsuspicious of the thunderstorm of the impeachment, which was soon to break forth from the gathering cloud in the forked lightnings of Burke's impassioned eloquence. The glory of the English name, since the battle of Plassey, was on the lip of every Hindu in Bengal, not that the irresistible unclean *M'lech'has* of the West were loved for themselves, for their very shadow was pollution, but only because they had come as deliverers from the licentious wrong and the hateful oppression of centuries of Mussulman misrule. The state of society into which she was ushered was so peculiar and exceptional in all its phases, that anything like it had never existed elsewhere, and nothing like it will ever exist anywhere again. The contemptuous tyranny and injustice of Islam had compressed Hindu society within itself to its utmost, and had condensed all the vapours of the traditional superstition into densest, darkest clouds. The triumph of caste—that impersonal incarnate demon-god, of the Hindu—over individual humanity and freedom, was complete. Sanskrit learning had sunk to its lowest ebb, and only guarded its reputation by the impenetrable mystery which it flung around its possessions. The millions were living like "dumb, driven cattle," ground down by physical miseries almost unparalleled in history, dependent entirely upon the selfish caprice of their tyrants, without the protection of law in their best doings, and helplessly exposed to the fellest ravages of famine and disease. Intellectual enlightenment was as much unknown as the conditions of a free, moral life. English was only acquired by a few as a means of verbal intercommunication and gain, but with no thought or desire after its literature and science. All the knowledge of the intellectual Hindu was still confined to the monstrous errors and absurdities of the Purans, and civilised men were still living their lives, four centuries after Copernicus, in utter ignorance of the real world around them. The imagination was filled to overflowing with the " gorgons, hydras and chimæras dire" of the old superstitious dreams ; and the will to do was suppressed by the terrorism of countless hells, compared with whose horror the descriptions of Dante's Inferno are as visions of Paradise. According to the science, " falsely so called," of the time, the earth was " shaped like the flower of the water-lily in which the petals project beyond each other." As it has been put in its most favourable light by Horace Hayman Wilson, the strongest of all the patrons of Sanskrit wisdom : " The Puranas distribute the earth into 7 concentric circles or rings, each forming an annular continent, and being separated from the next by a circumambient ocean. These oceans vary also as to their constituent parts ; and besides seas of fresh and salt water, we have them of treacle, honey, milk and wine. The whole is encompassed by a stupendous mountain belt, beyond which lies the religion (region ?) of darkness, and in the centre of all, which is also the centre of the continent we inhabit, towers Mount Meru, to the height of 64,000 miles." Or as it has been put in the celebrated minute by Macaulay, whose keen, shining pen, like Ithuriel's spear, lightly touched the demon of lies still in this earthly Eden " squat like a toad, close at the ear of Eve, Assaying by his devilish arts to reach The organs of her fancy, and with them forge Illusions as he list, phantasms and dreams"—the science of India consisted of "medical doctrines which would disgrace an English farrier, astronomy which would move laughter in girls at an English boarding school, history abounding with kings 30 feet high and reigns 30,000 years long, and geography made up of seas of treacle and seas of butter." Into this "dungeon horrible," in which so many fallen and degraded souls lay darkly bound, there yet streamed no ray of pure truth, no light illumed it, "but rather darkness visible served only to discover sights of woe." No Protestant missionary had yet ventured to set foot in Bengal in 1783. Still ten years had to pass before the sails of the *Princess Maria*, like angel wings, brought William Carey up the bay, with tidings of Divine peace and good-will to men, and other seven before the first soul was won to Christ, in the first year of the nineteenth century, from among the lost, prodigal millions. The new mercenary mercantile Government could not wholly alienate its English sense of justice, but its highest aim was merely how to press "*money*," "*more money*," and "*still more money*" out of the most impoverished peasantry in the world; and it was 13 years more before it would allow the all-revealing light of Divine Truth and Righteousness to shine forth into this gloom of human suffering and oppression. Such a tide of inhuman wrong and falsehood through "man's inhumanity to man"—shall certainly never return in this India again.

The changes of the past century in India have

indeed, been wonderful ; but like the web of life in general, and as was to be expected, they have been of "mingled good and ill together." The whole movement may be read in the light of history as a social struggle between the progressive spirit of an enlightened foreign philanthropy, and the blind inertia of a dogged internal resistance to change. In the last resort, it really resolves itself into a conflict between the ennobling religion of a Christ-like humanity and the degrading idolatry of caste. Looking at the work of the century as a whole, its selfish politics, its economic stagnation, its intellectual obscurantism, its occasional frensy of revolt, and its timid gropings after secular enlightenment, may all be understood in the light of this central relation. The conflict on its Hindu side has turned largely around the Sobha Bazaar family, the acknowledged head of the Hindu community ; and its salient points might be seen along the line of the personal recollection of "the celebrated old lady." Her boy-husband's grandfather, the famous Maharaja Nobo Krishna Deb, the founder of the house, was Persian Secretary to Lord Clive, and may have been with him not only at Plassey but afterwards at Moorshedabad, when, according to his own words, he walked, with moderate desires, through the treasury "with heaps of silver and gold to the right hand and to the left, and these crowned with jewels." Nobo Krishna did not make the mistake of the unprincipled and ill-fated Nuncoomar ; with more wisdom and less ambition, he recognised the invincibility of the new Power, and the family has always been honourably distinguished by its loyalty to the English Government. Great were the celebrations at Sobha Bazaar after the victory of Plassey ; greater still were they a hundred years later when a solid peace had crowned the madness of the mutiny. The *shradh* of the great Maharaja was on such a splendid scale that, according to my friend Shib Chunder Bose, in his excellent book, *The Hindoos as they are* : " To this day, it stands unrivalled in this city. Four sets of gold and sixty four sets of silver utensils, amounting to near a lakh of rupees, were presented as *dansagor* ( ocean-like gift ) upon the occasion. Besides these presents in money to Brahmins, upwards of two lakhs of rupees were given to the poor." Alas ! " Nature brings not back the mastodon," and the Maharanee never looked upon its like again ; and even her own magnificent *shradh* a few days ago, is a proof how all this idolatrous splendour is rapidly declining. But the greatest subject of boast of the old lady was no doubt her distinguished relative, Sir Radha Kant, the pride of the family and the great Coryphæus, amid Western enlightenment, of modern Hinduism. Born in the same year as herself, she may have watched his gradual growth in knowledge and superstition,—his patient pursuit of learning, his stern resolve to cling to all the old ways, his conservative contempt for the new life, and his strange illogical belief in the compatibility of secular instruction, even in women, with an honest adhesion to the ancestral creed. One of his enthusiastic admirers has called him, notwithstanding his very limited natural capacity, "the greatest of modern Hindus"; a eulogium which may well be disputed by the followers of the much nobler Raja Ram Mohun Roy. The greatness of Sir Radha Kant—if greatness it can be called—lay in what is most superficial in the achievements of thought and of life. He has left nothing behind him which all will recognise as a benefit, except his *Sabdakalpa-drama*—the hugest of Sanskrit Lexicons, and the work of many laborious years. Although he stood for half-a-century in the forefront of Hindu society, and had the grandest opportunities, he accomplished nothing for it of lasting good, notwithstanding his advocacy of female education according to the old type, and his co-operation with the secular reformers of his time. On all the great questions that affected the real progress of his countrymen, he was fatally and blindly wrong. The frantic advocate of *Suttee*, of *Polygamy*, of the extremest slavery of *Caste*, and of *Christian persecution* in the only form in which it was possible to him, will hardly be regarded as the loftiest style of man by the coming generations, and these he would have regarded as his chief claims upon their gratitude and veneration. Let us hear what a competent biographer says of him, as it has been recently edited by his more enlightened, if less erudite son, Raja Rajendra Narayan Bahadoor, who it may be allowed to believe, with all just family pride in his name, has yet recognised his fatal errors, and is not indisposed even to atone to posterity for the harm they have done.

"The superstitious element which had been mild in his father, Raja Gopeemohun and torpid in his uncle, Raja Rajkissen, assumed in him an aggressive development. It is, therefore, not to be wondered at, that his attachment to the antiquated usages of his country was as devoted, as his advocacy of educational measures was zealous. His belief in the wisdom of his ancestors was unlimited. Thus impressed, he proved during the latter end of his life an anachronism. Though naturally a humane man, his humanity was cramped by a mistaken prejudice for the institution of *suttee.* When Lord William Bentinck passed his celebrated edict for the abolition of that revolting rite, Radha Kant Deb moved the *Dhurma Sobha* to petition her Majesty's Government at home for the repeal of the same. Ram Mohun Roy was in England when the petition reached its destination, and had the gratification to see its prayer rejected. When the *Lex Loci* was passed by the Legislature of India, Radha Kant Deb not only failed to appreciate the great principle affirmed and recognised by it, but denounced it as an infringement of the rights of the Hindus. Great was his astonishment, greater still his indignation, when, on examining the provisions of the law, he found that native Christian converts, always his *bête noir*, were entitled to succeed to their inheritance when their fathers died intestate. He went up to her Majesty's Government for its abrogation. Happily for the interests of humanity, the petition shared the same fate as the *suttee* petition. Again in 1856, the Association of Friends for the Promotion of Social Improvement submitted to the Legislative Council a well-reasoned petition for the enactment of a law for the suppression of the evils of *Polygamy.* Radha Kant thought it proper to head a counter-movement, and get up a counter-petition. When he took action in these matters, he no doubt believed he was acting according to the dictates of his own conscience, but he was in reality exercising a retrogressive influence upon society... The views and dogmas of Radha Kant Deb marred his usefulness and interfered with the formation of a healthy public opinion. As the Coryphœus of Hinduism, his position was necessarily that of a patron of error. The circle in which he moved, and of which he was the centre, strove to ostracise enlightened men and to strangle reformatory measures. His religious drill-sergeant, Baboo Abinash Gangooly, exceeded his chief in the severity of his persecution of heterodoxy, and compelled him to war with heretics against his better judgment."

My quotation from this interesting writer has run out to such length that a regard for your valuable columns constrains me to reserve the conclusion of my letter till to-morrow. Meanwhile, let me commend this *rechauffage* of their early memories and traditions to my Hindu readers, in the full conviction that their judgment upon the efforts and policy represented by Sir Radha Kant will, every time their attention is earnestly turned to them, come into closer agreement with that of his appreciative and impartial biographer.

W. HASTIE.

The General Assembly's Institution,
October 1, 1882.

---

## THE SOCIAL CHANGES OF A CENTURY IN INDIA.

*(Continuation.)*

TO THE EDITOR.

SIR,—Faithful to his ingrained superstition unto the end, and a striking illustration of the "ruling passion strong in death," Sir Radha Kanta Deb, in 1867, in his eighty-fourth year, retired to the fragrant groves of Brindabun, there to die in the midst of scenes hallowed to his faith by the amatory sports of his tutelary god, Krishna, with the sixteen thousand *Gopis.* Altogether a remarkable phenomenon, in the latter half of the nineteenth century, even in this remarkable India. When we survey the work and the close of his life, many historical parallels rise into view; but we shall certainly never look upon his like again. In many points the industrious Sanskrit lexicographer might be compared with the great lexicographer of England, whose light was just going out when his was being kindled. Both had the same passion for verbal erudition, the same severe habit of self-discipline, the same honesty of conviction, the same traditional bigotry, the same distinction of intellectual vigour among their contemporaries. But Samuel Johnson's superstition was only an accident on the strong moral basis of his Christianity, and did no harm to any one; whereas Sir Radha Kanta's morality was an accident on the weak, filthy foundation of his superstition, and drove him almost unconsciously to all the harm that lay within his power. It would be hardly out of the proportions of history to compare him, in his kindred surroundings and aims, with the celebrated Julian the Apostate, whom he most resembled of all the great figures of antiquity. To him and his coadjutors may well be applied what has been recently said of Julian and his party, that they "were the Ultramontanes of their day in matters of religion, and the Romantics in matters of literature." Their social circumstances and problems were practically the same. In his time, as in Julian's, though as yet less powerfully, "those radical innovators, the Christians, were marching from conquest to conquest over the old faith, making no concealment of their revolutionary aims and their intentions to wipe out the past as speedily as possible. The conservatives of those times, after long despising the reformers, passed easily to fearing them and hating them as their success became threatening. 'The attachment to Paganism,' says Neander, 'lingered especially in many of the ancient and noble families of Greece and Rome.' Old families, or new rich ones who wished to be thought old, were sure to take up the cause of ancestral wisdom as against modern innovation." So it was with the pagan reaction of Radha Kanta Deb, exactly in principle and motive, if not in method or power, as it was with that of Julian. And the failure of the Hindu reactionary is now as conspicuous to all who have eyes to see the present movement, as was the case with his Roman prototype. We may almost wonder if the Genius of India did not rise before the closing inward eye of this latest national devotee, as the Genius of the empire is said to have risen before Julian on the fatal eve of his last battle, "covering his head and his horn of abundance with a funereal veil." Was he not, even in his last hour of apparent calm, when whispering to his attendants those learned instructions about the burning of his body with the sacred *tulsi*, and the feeding of turtles with its unconsumed remains, embittered by the consciousness of the false aims of his life and its ignominious failure, so as even to cry out in a last agony, 'Vicisti, Galilæe,' 'Thou hast conquered, O Galilæan!" Well might it have been so at least, and if history be indeed "philosophy teaching by examples," surely his descendants and his admirers will be warned by the lesson of his life.

The venerated Dowager Maharanee carried forward the traditions of the family, in living continuity, till to-day. And I presume that she also clung to the last, with all the fanaticism of her sex, to the ancestral faith. With a living husband she may have shared with her distinguished relative his pitiless enthusiasm for the supposed chastity of the fire-baptism of the *suttee*, and may have had her own intelligence brightened by an education beyond her peers; but we can hardly suppose that her womanly instinct did not revolt from his Mohammedan advocacy of polygamy. The great trial of her closing years must have been the daily increasing contrast in her experience, between the times that are and the times that were, and if the sunset of life gave her mystical lore, the shadow of coming events must have lain dark upon her soul. The increasing abandonment by every new generation of the old ways of life, and their wild rush ever more and more into all the forbidden paths, may have been the greatest grief of her last hours, as it is of all the orthodox contemporaries whom she has left behind. The visible disintegration of Hindu society, the contemptuous disregard of caste, the open contumely poured everywhere upon the old gods, may have but too evidently confirmed the low sad moan of the Brahman Gurus that the *Kali Yug*, the black "iron age" of universal degeneracy, indeed had come. And if there be in all Sanskrit literature anything approaching a prophecy of the present, it must, in the eyes of every conservative Hindu, be these remarkable words of the great Vishnu Purana :—

> Hear what will happen in the Kali age,
> The usages and institutes of caste,
> Of order and of rank will not prevail,
> Nor yet the precepts of the triple Veda.
> Religion will consist in wasting wealth ;
> In fasting and performing penances
> At will ; the man who owns most property,
> And lavishly distributes it, will gain
> Dominion over others ; noble rank
> Will give no claim to lordship ; self-willed women
> Will seek their pleasure, and ambitious men
> Fix all their hopes on riches gained by fraud.

And if saddened and overwhelmed by such experiences, she had been able to turn to the past for light and guidance amid her darkness, and yet in obstinate prejudice had turned away from the only Book that could clearly explain it all, she might have found something of such in the great historical parallel of the past to her own country and time. No student of history can fail to be struck with the extraordinary resemblance between the period of the decline and fall of Paganism in the Roman empire and what has been going on during the past century in India, and is in most vigorous movement to-day. "History indeed repeats itself," according to the law of similar causes being invariably followed by similar effects, and in this record of the first four Christian centuries in the ancient world of the West, we have given the outline of the future fate of India. To go no deeper even than Gibbon, the powerful anti-Christian historian of the Decline and Fall, the Hindu student will find in his brilliant chapters—on the religious condition of the empire in the time of the Antonines, the irresistible spread of the new religion even through blood and fire, the conversion of Constantine justly surnamed the Great, the ignominious failure of the romantic Apostate and the final destruction of Paganism in the reign of Theodosius,—more practical and instructive wisdom than in all the millions of dreamy stanzas in the Sanskrit literature. Again, I say, the classical student of Greece and Rome sees all that ancient past in the present of India again. Does not this sound as if it had been written by some agnostic historian of the Imperial Government and of the religious condition of India to-day?—

"The policy of the Emperor and the Senate, as far it concerned religion, was happily seconded by the reflections of the enlightened, and by the habits of the superstitious part of their subjects. The various modes of worship which prevailed in the Roman world were all considered by the people as equally true; by the philosopher as equally false; and by the Magistrate as equally useful . . . The Greek, the Roman, and the Barbarian, as they met before their respective altars, easily persuaded themselves, that under various names and under various ceremonies, they adored the same deities . . . The philosophers, viewing with a smile of pity and indulgence, the various errors of the vulgar, diligently practised the ceremonies of their fathers ; devoutly frequented the temples of the gods ; and sometimes condescending to act a part on the theatre of superstition, they concealed the sentiments of an Atheist under sacerdotal robes. It was indifferent to them what shape the folly of the multitude might choose to assume ; and they approached with the same inward contempt and with the same external reverence, the altars of the Lybian, the Olympian, or the Capitoline Jupiter."

I must refer my Hindu readers to the picturesque pages of Gibbon themselves for his graphic but dispassionate descriptions of the spread of licentiousness and corruptions of every kind with the decay of the old faith, which, according to a Roman authority, was so complete that the priests themselves when they gathered around the altars, and caught each others' eyes, could scarcely keep their countenance. To those who may only see the black cloud over the waste and despair of human life in the old empire, without catching a glimpse of the Divine glory gradually shining through, the historic parallel can, indeed, bring no comfort or faith ; and the prospect before them here, as before the Pagan patricians of Rome, can be only one of gloom and dismay. And this, it is to be feared, is the melancholy condition into which the proud hopes of thousands of the devout fathers and mothers of modern India are sinking fast, before the dread, inevitable mystery of the time.

The educated men of India, however, with a

higher wisdom, although not yet the highest, are no longer lamenting over the great social changes of the century, but are rightly rejoicing in them as a present possession and as the harbingers of still higher liberty and light. To them, as to all the merely human reformers in whose footsteps they would tread, ancient simplicity and faith are again upon the wing, and will soon restore the glories of their dream of the golden age. The great circle of the golden year will clasp the future to the past, and the wasting shapes of old disease will soon die and pass away. With the great poet who in this century has most musically echoed the classical spirit of India and Greece, they would sing—

> "The golden age begins anew,
> The golden years return,
> The earth doth like a snake renew
> Her winter weeds outworn.
> Heaven smiles, and faiths and empire gleam
> Like wrecks of a dissolving dream."

The hope is well and the effort is well, but "the half" is *not* really "greater than the whole"; and it may be allowed in all sincerity and earnestness to point out that whole. Believing with them, notwithstanding all the overt despairing Pessimism of the time, that a true life is still "worth the living," and believing also that the golden age is indeed beginning in a higher sense than theirs under Heaven's smile in this India, but that it will not unfold to its fulness without the more earnest co-operation of enlightened men, I shall venture, in my next letter, to point out some of the reasons which now may be urged more forcibly upon the acknowledged leaders of the Hindu community, to increase their certainty and to quicken their pace in the march of social reform.

W. HASTIE.

The General Assembly's Institution,
October 1, 1882.

Note.—This will close the series of Mr. Hastie's letters. Besides the replies to them which have been published, a number of others—some of them very lengthy—are now on our table, and a selection from them will be published as we find space available.—Ed., *S.*

## VI.

### A CLOSING WORD OF EXPLANATION AND APPEAL.

To the Editor.

Sir.—I hope you will allow me publicly to thank you for your kindness in granting me of late such large concessions of space for my letters on the Sobha Bazaar Rajbaree Shradh, which have been written solely from a sense of duty, in view of the facts publicly announced in your Report. I would also gratefully acknowledge the forbearance of your English Subscribers, who have borne without a murmur, and I hope not without some sympathy, these encroachments upon your principal page, although manifestly meant only for your Hindu readers. And I would not forget your other Correspondents who have contributed to the discussion, some of them kindly aiding me in my effort, and the others even in their bitterest antagonism shedding not a little light upon both the strength and the weakness of the present position of Hinduism. Above all, I wish to express my respect for the noble members of the Sobha Bazaar family, and the other distinguished participants in the ceremonial, who have given me the patient hearing I anticipated, and whose benevolent character remains of course unaffected by the reflections I have had to make upon their public practice and support of Idolatry. Had this been only a vulgar Shradh of unenlightened idolatrous Hindus, however ostentatious or magnificent, it would have passed entirely unnoticed by me; and I have only made it the theme of remark in the hope of quickening these honourable men to a consciousness of their false position in the eyes of the English world, and even of rousing them to assume their proper function as the enlightened and progressive leaders of the Hindu community in the great incumbent duty of religious and social reform.

The personal and polemical character of some of my utterances, although all founded upon material put before the world by the Sobha Bazaar family, might have required some slight apology, had their whole aim not been consciously conciliatory and irenic throughout. The *destructive* side of my argument was inevitable from the logical relations of the case, before I could enter upon any *constructive* effort with the anticipation of anything like ultimate agreement. The problem of the relation of our English enlightenment to the traditional Idolatry, which I raised at starting, has as yet been only half looked at; and I regret to learn that you cannot allow me to go on with a discussion of the burning question of *Social Reform in India* from my point of view, which is logically necessary in order to give completeness and justification to my discussion of the Hindu Idolatry. If you will not reconsider your decision, I must take an early opportunity of otherwise bringing my views under the consideration of your Hindu friends, not only because I believe I have something to say upon this subject which has not been said to them at least in public for some time, but because I wish to shew how thoroughly I am at one with them, as a Missionary, in every effort that aims at the real good of their country. Before leaving the discussion, however, at its present stage, I beg as a final favour that you will give me room for a closing word of general explanation to my critics, and of practical appeal to the enlightened patrons of the Shradh.

1. The acknowledged necessity of Social Reform in India has virtually been the common platform of all my reasoning with the educated Hindu, regarding the irreligiousness and inefficacy of the national Idolatry. So far at least we are agreed, upon the basis of his own professed conviction and upon my counter-experience of the benefits of the free, reformed English commonwealth ; and in this we are at one with the Government of India and with all the friends of the well-being of her people. And with our implicit agreement upon the irrationality of Idolatry, the only question upon which we differ is as to the best *method* of this necessary Social Reform. He is an advocate of an *indirect* method whose chief elements are secular education and liberal legislation, believing that these will, in the long run, bring out the result he professedly aims at. On the other hand, I am an advocate of a *direct* method of dealing with the cause of all the social deterioration and retardation of India, as being at once more philosophical and more practical, and as also inclusive of all the elements of his method. It must not be supposed that I have been as yet

endeavouring to prove the absolute truth of Christianity as the Divine religion, or that I am "under the delusion"—as one of your correspondents puts it —"of thinking that one or two letters will convert the educated Hindus into Christianity." That most difficult process would involve a purely theological discussion for which your columns can neither give me the facility nor admit the means required, according to my own conception of the Christian argument. My aim from the outset has merely been to get Christianity fairly looked at in its social and reformatory aspects, and to set it forth subsequently as the only thorough, safe, and effective means of Social Reform in India. Only thus far do I crave a hearing for its claims at present in this connection, on the part of educated Hindus, for their own sakes and that of their countrymen in general. It was not my intention to enter in your columns—even if you would allow me—upon an exposition or an apology of its higher spiritual mysteries. These might be referred to incidentally in so far as they were involved in or auxiliary to my argument; but the educated Hindu who still rejects them, can only argue against me logically from a proof of the social worthlessness or incapacity of Christianity, as a reforming agency. Joining with me in repudiating and denouncing the evils of the traditional Idolatry, his range of positive defence must be limited to a plea for its toleration, in the meantime, as a political expediency; or as theoretically justifiable on some philosophical view of his own. Arguments in reply against the religious or rational truth of Christianity are, therefore, really irrelevant to my contention. Even if it could be shewn—which it certainly cannot—that Christianity is as groundless a superstition as Hinduism, and that all the particular arguments that overthrow the philosophy of the one are likewise applicable to the doctrines of the other, my practical appeal would still remain. As I see it, the usual "tu quoque" retort of the educated Hindu upon the Christian Advocate, is not only prompted by an altogether erroneous motive from ignorance of the historical origin and practical aim of Christianity, but it is entirely vicious as a reply from being founded upon a complete misunderstanding of the theology of the Christian system. If I had not the terrible examples of all the other religions of the ancient world, and especially of the twin religions of Greece and Rome before me, the same rejoinder might perhaps be given to my arguments by the Hindu Apologist. Had he before him the universal social failure of Christianity, or of any religion akin to it in ancient or modern times, he *might* urge something for the ancient Hinduism he still would fain have us reverence, although its light and life have gone out in his own head and heart. But Christianity is still as vital and elevating as ever it was in the lives of men, and is most visibly advancing with an ever accelerating movement to the spiritual conquest of the whole world. In every age, it has had its opponents and doubters, but these were never really so feeble or ineffective as now. Although a dozen of such blustering sciolists, who have spent what intellectual energy they had in other departments of enquiry, may be cited in loose and pretentious writing upon the philosophy of the Christian religion, their names will be forgotten in fifty years, but the great facts of Christendom will still survive, and what is more striking, will survive even the errors and weaknesses of its present representatives. Christianity has not only been the real civiliser of Europe, but is still the chief power in all the social reform and progress of the age. Surely, then, there is no Hindu so highly educated yet, as not to be willing to listen to her earnest voice, nor so unpatriotic as not to pause betimes and calmly consider whether this be not indeed God's own remedy at last, however accompanied with human imperfection, for all the evils and sufferings of his country. This is, of course, my own faith, and I believe that I am able to shew—and yet hope to shew—that it is established by all the available resources of philosophy, history and science, if we will only open our eyes to their light and our hearts to their power.

I must reluctantly reserve till to-morrow, my practical appeal to the enlightened patrons of the Shradh.

W. HASTIE.

The General Assembly's Institution.
October 10, 1882.

## CONCLUSION OF LAST LETTER.

2. If anything in what has been already said about the Hindu Idolatry has given pain to any in whom there still lingers some faint regard for the old gods, they must at least recognise that it was absolutely necessary for the logical exigencies of my argument, and it may even be acknowledged that it has been done in the spirit of the physician who probes the sore to the bottom that he may find a radical cure for the disease. Such, indeed, is the state of the case that no discussion regarding the reform of Hindu Society, that attempts to deal with first principles and primary causes, can possibly pass over the subject of the traditional Idolatry. For, as we all know, it so completely pervades the whole social structure and movement of Hindu life, that it meets the Reformer as his chief obstacle at every turn, and no effort in the direction of progress can possibly be made without coming into conflict with it in practice. My cardinal objection to all the indirect methods of Reform referred to, is that they have not the courage to look facts in the face, and like all quack remedies founded upon a superficial diagnosis, they accordingly "but skim and film the ulcerous part, While rank corruption mining all within, Infects unseen." I claim, therefore, to be not only honest and straightforward, but to proceed upon an intelligible principle, that looks at once at causes and means and ends in its survey, and to be as exempt from personal considerations, as it is possible to be, in my advocacy of the cause of Righteousness and

Truth. And if I am heard out it will be seen that I shall be neither so extreme nor so unpractical in my suggestions, as may be anticipated. And once for all I declare that, if I have said anything that is in the least untenable regarding the Hindu Idolatry, I shall always be ready to withdraw it whenever my error is shewn.

But apart altogether from the ultimate truth or falsehood of the Hindu system, its social evils remain as undeniable facts. It is evident even from the most cursory review of the changes of the past century, that the progress of Society in India has been in the inverse ratio of the resistant power of idolatrous Caste, and in the direct proportion of the introduction of the spiritual energy of the Christian civilisation. If there be any truth in historical generalisation at all, this is an elementary and indisputable induction. The extraordinary persistent opposition offered to all the efforts made to improve the condition of the people,—to utilise more largely the natural resources of the country, to introduce the necessities and advantages of modern civilised life, to promote a freer social relationship among the different classes of the people, to diffuse the light of a beneficent education, and even to mitigate the sufferings arising from famine and disease,—has proved the utterly abnormal condition of Hindu Society in too superabundant detail. And as yet, the real source of all the social misfortunes of India has, with the sole exception of the Missionary effort, been approached or attacked only from the outside and in its effects, as if it were enough to deal with a symptom in trying to remove the cause of a fatal disease. Further, these indirect methods are still superficial, hesitating, and slow ; and, as in view of a sufferer in the very agony of dissolution whose sufferings may yet be stayed and whose waning life may yet be restored, I feel constrained to appeal in behalf of this suffering people, to the enlightened leaders of native society, for more fundamental, earnest, and vigorous action in the cause of progress and reform.

Yes, it is to you, my friends—if you will allow me so to address you, in the spirit of Christian faith and hope and love—it is to YOU, in the responsible position in which Providence has placed you and in the clear noon-day of the English Enlightenment which is now your pride, that we may well turn with an *Appeal* for aid, in our warfare with the idolatry which is still degrading the mass of your countrymen and indirectly ruining the spiritual life of your sons. I believe that you have as little faith in it as I have ; and that you only lack the courage to be true to your convictions, and the spiritual impulse that can alone inspire that courage. I address you as men animated by a stronger love of your country than a stranger like me can pretend to, and well qualified to judge of what is really for its good. And my closing word of Appeal shall only be an indication of the grounds upon which any participation on your part in the popular Idolatry, seems to me to be unjust to your less enlightened countrymen and unworthy of yourselves.

(1) And, first of all, I appeal against all support of Idolatry, whether by personal participation or countenance, to your own *enlightened Reason and Conscience.* This was the main argument, as I have stated, that was addressed by St Paul to the intellectual men of ancient Athens, and it is surely even more relevant to you to-day, for you have the history of more than other eighteen centuries to prove and strengthen its force. One of the great Fathers and Apologists of the Christian Church philosophically regards the human mind as *naturally Christian,* and as spontaneously giving its testimony to Divine Truth (*testimonium animae naturaliter Christianae.*) This consciousness of the inherent nobleness of human nature, is what gives its name and character to the Aryan race. But the sensual degradation of Idolatry is an essential contradiction of this inherent nobility of spirit and must be consciously felt by you to be so, if the old Aryan dignity still survives in your souls. Away with it then, and on the ground of an honourable self-respect alone, be done with it henceforth. Be assured that every concession you make to the traditional Idolatry, degrades you in the eyes of all the other members of the Aryan race—be they Parsi or Greek or German or English—who have now all escaped from its degrading thraldom.

(2) Again, I appeal against the present Idolatry to the original non-idolatrous Religion of the Hindu race. " *The Vedic Hindus never worshipped Idols.*" This position has been pressed upon you

by an enlightened band of native Reformers from the days of Ram Mohun Roy, who wrote with a learning abreast of his age: "The Vedas hold out precautions against forming a Deity after human imagination and recommend mankind to direct all researches towards the surrounding objects, viewed either intellectually or individually, bearing in mind their regular, wise, and wonderful combinations and arrangements." This view is now held by every competent scholar without exception; and with the dying out of the passionate clinging to the idol, may surely become your creed too. "The religion of the Vedas" says Max Müller, "knows of no Idols. The worship of idols in India is a secondary formation, a later degradation of the more primitive worship of ideal gods." Similarly one of your own young scholars says: "We find no resemblance between modern Hinduism and the Vaidik religion... From a careful examination of the Vedas, we find that modern Hinduism has little or no affinity with the Vaidik religion, *The Vaidik Hindus never worshipped idols.*" Very incongruous and startling was it, then, to read in the report of the great *Shradh* that the idolatrous worship of the idol *Gopinathjee,* was brought to a close by "all the Brahmans present pronouncing the Vedic benediction." If this was meant to give anything like a semblance of Vedic dignity to the idolatrous ceremonial, it was an entire blunder, and was a proof only of utter ignorance or of sheer imposture on the part of the Brahmans. I prefer to take the former alternative, and as I have already set them one problem which is likely to try all their wits for some time to come, let me set them another which is at least within the reach of their patient verbal industry. I assert that the Vedas nowhere give any countenance to the modern Idolatry of the Shradh; and I challenge them to produce a single text in which *Shraddha* is referred to as a ceremony or as more than a mere personification of the virtue of reverence or filial piety. *The Shradh has no more Vedic authority on its side than Suttee had.* This position too is now being recognised by native scholars, as, for instance, by the learned Professor Sarvadhikari in his able treatment of the principles of the Hindu Law of Inheritance, in his recent Tagore Lecture. But the challenge may, as every student of Hinduism knows, be extended very much further. I therefore challenge the Brahmans, at the same time, to find a single text in the Vedas that would go to establish the existence even of Gopinath-jee or Krishna and the new Vaishnav ritual, or of Shiva—Rudra "the howler" notwithstanding—and the Linga, or of Durga and her Puja, or of the whole Shakti faith and worship, or even of caste as an original Aryan institution, notwithstanding the faint signs of it creeping into the Purusha Sukta and one or two more of the very latest Hymns. But these constitute the very sum and substance of modern Brahmanism, although there is not a trace of them except the last, in the whole of the Vedas. Well, then, might the young scholar referred to, write; "We find *no resemblance* between modern Hinduism and the Vaidik religion." But the Vedas are to the Hindu, the ultimate standard of authority and appeal, in all matters of religion. I appeal, therefore, from these modern aberrations to your own Divinest Scriptures; and if the Brahmans cannot face this appeal, let them give up their claim to be Brahmans, and do you likewise give up the whole modern Idolatry to its inevitable ruin and collapse.

(3) It is only a continuation of the same line of argument, when I further appeal against this Idolatry to *the whole history of Hinduism*, in order to shew its An-aryan orgin and nature, and the corrupting influence which it has exercised upon the primitive religion of your first forefathers. On this question, also, the great Sanskrit scholars are now generally agreed, although there are still differences among them on some points in detail. All of them now hold that Shiva and Durga and the other later gods that are worshipped by Idols, were *not* the Divinities of the Aryan conquerors at all, but of the pre-Aryan inhabitants of India and that they are thus essentially of *a Sudra origin and character.* Upon this complicated and difficult question, without entering on the discussion of theories, it may here suffice to remind you that it has now been made out, that the first invaders of India were of the black Hamitic race, who certainly spread from Egypt to Babylonia over the south of Asia, and who in all probability entered India from the West before the original Babylonians were conquered by the Shemites

and the Aryans. Some of the lowest tribes in India may still be regarded as the lineal representatives of this original stock. However the blaker elements in the population of Southern India and Malaysia may be related to these Nigritian or Cushite immigrants, it seems clear that they had established themselves in Aryavarta before the Aryan invasion, had developed a rude material civilisation of their own, and had even introduced their coarse naturalistic worship among the Dravidian settlers of the Dekhan. Philological researches have established the ethnological difference between them and the Dravidians (including the Tamil, Telugu, Canarese, and Malayalam branches) and the so-called Aboriginal tribes of northern India (including the Kols, the Santhals and others); and it is now held that both the latter are of Turanian origin, and that they entered India from central Asia by the North East or North West. When the white Aryan conquerors invaded India by the North West, they found these Hamitic and Turanian settlers in possession; and the Vedas and the great Epics give glimpses of the conflicts and the victories that ensued. The pre-Aryans were the Dasyus, the Rakshasas and the Asuras of the Vedas and of the Epics. Some at least of the Kolarians were the allies of Rama and appear as the monkeys with Hanuman at their head; and that yellowish race may, then or earlier, have occupied most of the Gangetic valley. The pre-historic relation between the Nigritians and Dravidians is very obscure, but it cannot be doubted that many of the former were driven to the hills of northern India, and most of the latter to southern India and Ceylon by the Aryan conquerors. But so far from being exterminated the pre-Aryan settlers, reduced to slavery, continued to form the bulk of the population, and their direct descendants and those of the mixed castes form at present about three fourths of the population of India. It was not merely a social necessity, but a political wisdom that incorporated them on the lowest level of the social scale, into the great Aryan commonwealth. And with them were absorbed all the elements of their low naturalistic religion, which gradually issued in the complete corruption and degradation of the old Aryan faith.

The philological and ethnological evidences in support of this view cannot be given here, but they are varied and increasing, and among them the descriptions of the negroid Rakshasas in the Ramayan will at once occur. But there is no more important or convincing evidence than what is furnished by the new science of Comparative Mythology. When we look at these closely we see that Shiva and Durga, with all their idol train, were neither the divinities of the non-idolatrous Aryans nor of the demon-worshipping Turanians, but were identical with the gods of the Western Hamites,—with the Babylonian Bal and Baaltis (Mylitta), the Asyrian Bel and Ishtar, the Phœnician Baal-Peor and Ashtaroth (Astarte), the Egyptian Kham and Athor (in the later forms Osiris and Isis) and even with the phallic and Aphrodisiac divinities of the Greeks, and the Priapus and Venus of the Romans. And if we go to the root of the matter we shall find that all these are only idolatrous or anthropomorphic modifications, arising from their mixture with higher types, of those lowest forms of sensual nature-worship which characterised the Hamitic substratum of the population of Southern and Western Asia. Left to itself its arbitrary and unconnected apprehension of tangible objects as individual sources of Divine power, everywhere degenerates into Fetishism, or the worship of accidental "stocks and stones." When its unbridled surrender to the animal life of nature is combined with the vivid personifications of the powers of nature by a higher and more intellectual race, the issue is sensuous image-worship and licentious ceremonialism. We see this process of corruption on a great scale in the history of the Shemitic religions of South Western Asia, where the original worship of supreme Power or Will sank down, with a single exception, to a grovelling idolatry. But we see it on an even greater scale in India, where the intellectual Aryan, who had at first lifted his face into the light of heaven and greeted the shining forms of nature as supernatural personalities akin to his own, lowered himself to the brute by abandoning his primitive majestic religion and taking on the grossest abominations of the once hated Barbarians. Here too, as in the case of Rome, the vanquished took their conquerors captive, and reduced them to the worse slavery of mere animalism and lust. If this view be correct, the modern Idolatry of Hinduism, as distinguished from the original Aryan religion, is a sensual degradation of the early ideal Polytheism by the absorption of the crass material Nature-worship of the lowest tribes. And as the element of mere sensual indulgence increased and the images of its types multiplied, the earlier gods were abandoned until their very names were frequently forgotten. The reaction from the abstract refinement of Buddhism, gave popularity and power to the coarse new gods, and their votaries were conciliated by the idolatrous homage paid to them by the old priests. The terrible Shiva cuts off a head of Brahma with his finger-nail ; and the supremacy of the Indian Kronos passes till hardly a Brahman could be found to do him honour. The hideous Durga takes the place of the fair-faced Ushas and Asvins ; and the melodious music of the Vedic hymns sinks into the swinish gruntings of the Purans. The transformation became complete ; and in his new An-aryan worship the Hindu Aryan lost the nobility of his manhood. And this is the very Idolatry of to-day : the faith of a degraded alien race, the cult of a knavish priesthood, the disgrace of the Hindu name. And surely this obscene barbarian worship is the vilest possible pollution of Aryan purity ; and I appeal against it to your own sense of veneration for the founders of your race, and your own claims to rank among the free fair Aryan peoples.

(4) Once more, I appeal against this idolatrous Hinduism to your own moral perception of its de-

grading influence upon the spiritual life of your country. It is chargeable with the moral ruin of India for a thousand years, and surely that is enough to condemn it in every patriotic mind. I shall not repeat what I have already said in my Third Letter regarding the demoralising influence of this Idolatry upon the individual life as we see it around us; but let me here add that the same result appears in equal degree in the other departments of the mental life of the people. Look at the gross ignorance and intellectual degradation of the masses, and you must acknowledge that it is the handiwork of the popular superstition alone. I do not merely refer to women, whom it has visibly degraded to immeasurable depths below their ancient high level, but to the national mind as a whole. It has been well put by a writer on the popular religion of India some time ago, and as his judgments were founded upon experience, I shall quote his words.

"The effects of Idolatry have been in this country, as everywhere else, *mental imbecility.* The intellect of the Hindu is crippled. Why? Not from any Bœotian influence in the atmosphere, but *because his religion requires the native to abjure the exercise of his reason.* Says the *Gita*, 'he who worships matter becomes matter,' *i. e.* a blockhead. Religion requires him to regard certain stones and certain trees as gods, but common sense teaches him to view them as they are. Religion overpowers common sense; the mind becomes stupified; and the man bows down to that block, which he himself, as a child, had perhaps often regarded as a plaything. He, in other respects, so nice and subtle as—to borrow an oriental expression—to split a hair in his reasonings, considers it an animated being, offers it food to eat and flowers to smell, clothes it in winter to keep it warm, and fans it in summer to allay the heat ! The rats and mice are more shrewd, says Brojomohun, a clever native, who published a masterly refutation of Polytheism,—than this human being, for they regard the wood *as* wood, and cut holes in it. Even the cockroaches spare it not, nor the goats and flies, for these eat up the colours wherewith it is painted. But the *man* still thinks that block a God, to which he himself gave mouth, nose and features, hands and feet. It can be burnt down with fire, broken into pieces by the hammer [and thrown by himself into the river], as well when a god as in its original condition. But this does not shake his strong belief. He fancies Him laughing, he dreams that he sees a frown ; and thus professing himself to be wise, he becomes a fool. What a sharp intellect, what a sound understanding is thus rendered imbecile by Superstition !"

In this grim, gloomy idolatry then, reigning as a King of Terror in India through the night of a thousand years, we have the explanation of the benighted condition of her people, the decay of her art, the gross ignorance of the masses, and the continuing puerility of even her best minds. For a thousand years India did not contribute a book worth reading to the literature of the world, nor add a single new idea to the thoughts of mankind. Such is the intellectual memorial of her Idolatry !

(5) Further, I appeal against this extravagant and wasteful Idolatry, to your own knowledge of *the principles of social Economy*, and its practical importance for the well-being and progress of the people. Our age is giving much of its intellectual interest to the study of this subject, and has raised it to the dignity of a science ; and it is beginning to receive

an intelligent appreciation even in India. As I said at the outset, I refrain from any special reference to the vast expenditure on this particular Shradh, and am now looking at the economic aspects of the subject in its widest range. I have nothing to say against anything that can truly adorn or sweeten the movement of human life, and have only sympathy for its nobler charities. I even recognise the desirability of timeous relaxation of the tension of modern life, and the importance of beautiful art and healthful joyousness as auxilary to its severest duties and highest aims. But a view of even a tithe of the useless waste of wealth and energy upon mere idol-worship in this India, with all these clamant and oppressive social wants alongside of it, would surely be enough to draw " iron tears " from the sternest political economist of the time. I feel the force of this relation most deeply at this moment as the horrid clang of preparations all around for the mad extravagant revel of the Durga Puja, rises loudly to my ears. The Government of India with all its beneficent efforts declares that it *cannot* educate the millions from want of means in this poor country ; and to the appeal of her generous Ruler for private aid in this great national duty, but a feeble and callous response comes from the millionaires. But the lascivious Krishna and the sanguinary Durga do not so plead in vain. "Oceans" of offerings are still poured on *their* altars ; and the shameless prostitutes who shine in the Nautch, are loaded with golden gifts wrung from the imbruted toil-worn ryot who cannot send his children to school. Can India ever become better while it is so, or lift up her "dejected head" again, among the nations ? Surely this appeal is practical enough, and far enough from the metaphysical subtleties of speculation, to command an earnest assent. I venture to affirm that what is wasted in mere idol-worship in India would even now *educate* the children of all the millions, and soon make India the first empire of the world. *With what will be thus laid upon the unholiest of shrines in Calcutta, during these three days alone, I would myself undertake during the next year to send the light of human knowledge and the life of Divine love into the homes of* A MILLION *of your countrymen.* This surely should give you pause amid these idolatrous revellings. Think not that we Missionaries have come here to oppose your progress, or to seek anything from you for ourselves. We know that all Idolatry is essentially unproductive and retrogressive; that it is utterly opposed to the whole industrial and mechanical movement of the age; and that no people can possibly rise to the level of modern civilisation and science, until it is removed from their midst. And on this ground alone, if we had no higher, we might justify our mission, and claim to be at one with every genuine effort put forth for the good of the people. It is for you to say whether we are not justified, in the light of the whole history of the civilisation of mankind, in protesting against all participation of educated men in the wasteful extravagance of Idolatry ; and whether, even apart from its more moral bearings, the idolatrous ceremonial is not an outrage on the enlightenment of the nineteenth century, as well as a wrong to your countrymen and yourselves. Were your Idolatry once for all removed, not an honest or healthful source of human enjoyment would be taken away, but the world around you would forthwith become brighter and better and the millions would learn to rejoice in a nobler humanity. And this consideration alone should surely make you pause; and consider whether the time has not now come for you as practical and earnest men, not only to "flee from" every form of idolatry, but even to take more practical steps for its utter abolition.

(6) But, finally, and as the chief of all my objections, I appeal from this ignoble and irrational Idolatry *as a Sin* against the Personality and Majesty of God, to *all your higher knowledge of His Divine truth about Himself as revealed in history.* If any devotee of mere Aryan culture should say that *this* is Hebraic fanaticism, I shall only reply that nothing could less truly be said of my faith, and that it is not in my method to ground this gravest of all considerations upon a mere positive command. But amid our solemnest responsibilities in life, and above all in matters of religion, the first rule of a sober English thinker was surely a wise one, "*Never go against the best light you have.*" It was, indeed, not only the faith, but the experience of the Hebrew people—and they remain as a living proof of it to-day—that all pub-

lic Idolatry was National Sin; and that the all-righteous God dealt with this revolt and apostacy from His supreme authority as being such. But it is not merely in the fates of the Hebrew people that we read this Revelation; all our "best light" regarding the universal Government of *God in History* establishes the same law. A great German writer, who would have been the last to do an injustice to India, has said in his own comprehensive way, "Who can deny depth of thought to the religious consciousness of India; and yet it must take a low place in the history of that of the race at large. *God in history is a point very little developed in the religion of the Indian races.*" No one can question the force of this pregnant remark, and all the more earnestly do I refer you to Universal History and to the new Philosophy of History—and not merely to the Bible although it is the very central faith of the Bible—for the proof that the Righteousness of God has been everywhere revealed, and not least visibly in this India, against the Sin of Idolatry. And we have seen into something of the reason, as we have found it always accompanied with a degradation of what is noblest and divinest in man. The great idolatrous empires that have successively arisen, and flourished for a day of time, and then passed away, have all proved that *Idolatry is essentially inconsistent with the moral order of the Universe.* And to-day, there is not an idolatrous people that holds a foremost place in the polity of nations. The blight of Idolatry is even unhappily to be found—as a correspondent has suggested—within the circle of Christendom itself; it is there as a survival of the idolatrous worship of Pagan Rome, and still its shadow spreads from the old imperial city. But *there* too, the Divine Will of Righteousness authenticates itself; and there is not a people who have fallen under the sway of the ancient Idolatry even in Christian forms, but is at this moment in the rear of spiritual progress and even of common civilisation. Read Macaulay's striking contrast of Catholic and Protestant Europe : and see whether even the professedly Christian votary of Idolatry is saved from the inevitable curse.

If, notwithstanding all this testimony from experience, you still say that it is *inconceivable* how mistaking a dead image for the living God and bowing down to it in this belief, *can* have any prejudicial influence upon the spiritual life of an individual or a people ; then let us look, in conclusion, at the relation of the Idolater to the Divine Will yet a little more closely. We have seen how Idolatry consists in putting an artificial image in place of the only living and true God, and then by a voluntary turn of the imagination regarding it as God Himself. The devotion of the genuine Idolater becomes limited to the form of his idol, and for the time he really sees nothing Divine beyond it. This is the real application of the recent theory of *Kathenotheism*, which does not seem to be applicable, in any very important sense, to the Vedic worship. But the Idol is after all, only a product of the Idolater as the work of his own head and hands, so that what is actually before him is but an objective representation of his own feeling or state of mind. Idolatry is thus at the best an inverted self-worship; and the Divine cannot rationally be held, even on Pantheistic grounds, to be more fully embodied in the Idol than in any other cognate material substance. For I at once discount the influence of the incantation of the priest, as a sham which modern enlightenment will no longer away with. In reality then the idolater, by an act of his own will, cuts himself off from the Divine Personality, and, sunk entirely within his own feeling, is never farther away from Divine influence than in the wildest delirium of his sensuous worship. It is no slight matter, then, to mistake a dead idol for the living God, if the living God be indeed the highest source of power to human life. No other mistake that may be made about finite things, *can* ever be so great or so detrimental as this; for it amounts to nothing less than voluntarily barring the approach of the Divine spirit to all the energies of the soul. Idolatry is thus the worst of all the practical lies, to which the soul of man can surrender itself.

From this point of view, we at once see the immediate cause of the spiritual deterioration, and of the ensuing moral degradation inseparably connected with idolatry. Choosing his own false way, by his own self-will, the Idolater alienates himself from the Divine Personality, and is left free to descend into the abyss to which it naturally leads. He even mistakes the impulses of his own flesh for the Divinest inspirations, and feeds his soul sweetly upon the very pabulum of spiritual death. In this voluntary estrangement of the self-will from the supreme Divine Will, consists the *sinfulness* of idolatry and and all the *evil* of the moral corruption that necessarily ensues.

And looking at it still further in its last resort, is it irrational to believe that God should demand the conscious and voluntary co-operation of Man, in working out His supreme purpose of salvation in humanity ? If He has made the world for man and man for His own highest glorification, it becomes rather inconceivable how this chief end of finite existence *could* be accomplished without the free activity of the individual in a consciousness of his true relation to the Divine. It is on this highest relation of humanity, that all Hindu Religion and Philosophy have fundamentally erred. The deepest Aryan thought failed to comprehend *how* there could be room in the universe along with the Infinite Absolute Will, for a free finite will ; and in the last gasp of a Pantheistic negation, sank down again to the level of merest animal life. But this is the deepest truth of the highest Revelation, and beside it the pallid form of Hindu speculation looks cold and lifeless indeed. God *will not*, nay *cannot*, give His own life to man against his will, nor in direct contradiction to the essential conditions of that Life. The Divine Self-consciousness cannot dwell in mere animal organisms ; and the circle of Being can only be consciously linked back again to God, in the finite spirits, that have been emancipated from their natural selves. And so it is not in the sensuous or abstract self-idolatry of Hinduism, but in the spiritual and voluntary self-sacrifice of Christianity, that the great religious mystery of the Universe is truly and finally disclosed.

I linger in search of a last word of irresistible power, anxious lest I may not yet have reached your sympathies, and afraid to leave such a momentous issue on any mere reasonings or expostulations of my own. And so I am driven at the last to *the Divine Law* itself, as the surest and the strongest of all the condemnations of Idolatry, and as fraught at once with the solemnest warning of Divine judgment and the most attractive encouragement of Divine mercy. However some may cavil, in a petty way, at the lightnings of Sinai "and the voice of the trumpet exceeding loud," the Historian can still see the great Commandments written as with letters of fire over all the onward march of humanity, and hear them sounding as in tones of thunder high over all the noise and terror of life, down through all the ages. And I pray that you may not, amid the idolatrous clamour all around, now miss their deep meaning and their strong message to yourselves.

"And God spoke all these words saying,

"THOU SHALT HAVE NO OTHER GODS BEFORE ME.

"Thou shalt not make unto thee any graven image, or any likeness of *anythiny* that is in heaven above, or that is in the earth beneath, or that is in the water under the earth:

"Thou shalt not bow down thyself to them nor serve them : for I the Lord thy God am a jealous God, visiting the iniquity of the fathers upon the children unto the third and fourth generation of them that hate me;

"And showing mercy unto thousands of them that love me, and keep my commandments."

"Wherefore" saith the great Apostle of the Gentiles, more than fifteen centuries afterwards to the idolatrous men of Corinth,—which of all ancient cities the most resembled this Calcutta of ours— "let him that thinketh he standeth, take heed lest he fall. There hath no temptation taken you but such as is common to man ; but God is faithful who will not suffer you to be tempted above that ye are able ; but will with the temptation also make a way to escape, that ye may be able to bear it. Wherefore" he tenderly concludes—in words which I shall affectionately appropriate as my last to you— "wherefore, my dearly beloved, *flee from Idolatry.* I SPEAK AS TO WISE MEN; JUDGE YE WHAT I SAY."

W. HASTIE.

The General Assembly's Institution,
First Durga Puja Day, 1882.

# APPENDIX.

# HINDU IDOLATRY

AND

# ENGLISH ENLIGHTENMENT.

## APPENDIX

CONTAINING CONTROVERSIAL LETTERS
UPON THE SUBJECT
BY HINDUS AND OTHERS.

*Reprinted from the Statesman,*

*September—November.*

1882.

## AUDI ALTERAM PARTEM.

Iron sharpeneth iron, so a man sharpeneth the countenance of his friend. As in water face answereth to face, so the heart of **man to man.**

Truth, like a Torch, the more it's shook it shines.

# APPENDIX.

## EXPLANATORY NOTE.

The following controversial Correspondence has been reprinted not only in order to give the other side a fair hearing, but because it furnishes a most interesting contribution to our means of estimating the intellectual strength and resources of contemporary Hinduism. It may be taken for granted that the Letters here reproduced were the best in the mass of Correspondence sent by natives to the Editor of the *Statesman* in defence of their Idolatry, or at least that they are fairly representative of what was sent. It appears from an Editorial Note, that the number of Letters written by Hindu Correspondents was very considerable. In his issue of 14th November the Editor says, "We published a few of the Letters sent to us, but the *rudis indigestaque moles* of manuscript still in our possession is so vast that we lack the time even to attempt to deal with it. We cannot even read it." Although this inability of the Editor may be regretted, yet all who know anything of the position from their own experience, will admit that the Letters actually printed give a fair statement of the case for Hinduism from various sides. The high literary quality of many of them, which will probably surprise most English readers, is a guarantee that much of the best available power of the Educated Hindus had been brought into the field, and this is conspicuously the case with *Ram Chandra*, the most notable of the controversial Correspondents. If any thing better or stronger *can* be said on the Hindu side, I for one would be glad to have it, because the Missionary in India has nothing to fear but everything to hope from candid discussion of the cardinal issue between Paganism and Christianity. I entirely differ from those who think the position is to be won for Christ in educated Hindu society, without further controversy. It would be contrary to all the past experience of the Church if it were so ; and least of all is there any such probability in this intellectual, dialectical, rhetorical India, where the chief danger is rather lest the awakening progressive mind may turn apathetically aside from Christianity and settle down, without further religious enquiry, into a cold indifferent Secularism. It is most important to catch the intellectual activity at this stage and to force it earnestly to face the momentous claims of the religious life ; and this is the very motive and purpose of our Missionary Colleges in which the intellectual movement is accompanied by a spiritualising and fertilising Christian influence all through. The chief duty and difficulty of the educational Missionary has always been to follow the Brahmanical system into all its intellectual retreats, and to drag it up into the clear convicting daylight of modern Science. And the chief obstacles to his success have been the obstinate prejudices, the pretentious self-certainty, the unreasoning arrogance, the fanciful infallibility, and the cuttle-fish artifices of the ingrained and closely organised Traditionalism. All this, however, is now nearly gone. The educational method—faithfully carried on in the General Assembly's Institution since 1830—has been doing its work, and Hinduism with the fierce light of the modern mind now beating upon all its ghastly excrescences and inner attenuations, is upon its last defence. The difficulty now is to find a fair and frank Defender who will maintain the system in its thoroughness or even keep to the question. On this account, the Letters here presented from Educated Hindus cannot fail to be read with interest, as shedding some light upon the present condition of the religious life of India, and with only an occasional hint or correction in a note, I shall leave them, from this point of view, to speak and to plead for themselves.

W. H.

November, 1882.

---

# LETTERS BY HINDUS AND OTHERS.

## I.—IDOLS AND DOLLS.

### To the Editor.

Sir,—Mr. Hastie's profound letter on the subject of Hindoo idolatry, which appears in your issue of this morning, will no doubt be appreciated by thinking minds ; while he has not left others without something for their good as well. His practical treatment of the argument from *dolls* is as telling as it is true. Yet there is room left to say a word or two on this aspect of the subject, which I should like, if you allow me, to fill up. My remarks will be of a common-place character ; but as an appeal to common sense and not to " supersensuous Reason," they will perhaps be more level to the ordinary capacity, than your learned correspondent's philosophical essay. " As you Europeans give *dolls* to *your* children ; so do we Hindoos give these *idols* to *our* children, to our uneducated women and common people, who cannot do without them." This from the mouth of a bigoted Brahmin ( such as I have known, and do know ) has both force and significance ; but from the lips of enlightened men like Sir Radha Kanta Deb, it looks exceedingly like a miserable evasion. The *essence* of the argument for idols, as illustrated by the example of dolls, is that the images of Kali, Doorga, Gunesh, Krishna, &c., with their scenery and surroundings, representing the *debtas* and the *debis*, give a sensible exhibition of the *life of the gods*. The imagery and the *jatras* bring the Hindoo heaven down to earth ; and make the invisible world of mythology comprehended by worshippers in flesh and blood. *Believe in the mythology of Hindooism*, and its idolatry becomes lit up with meaning. The argument of the sincere Brahmin is akin to the argument of the early Christian church for miracle-plays, which afforded instruction as to the facts of Gospel history and Old Testament biography, to people who could not read the Scriptures.

But it becomes a very different thing indeed to one who, like our educated Bengalees, have swept the entire mythology of Hindooism into the back side of the world, into that limbo large and wide, "since called *the paradise of fools.*" To such the whole system of idolatry must be lying, and calculated to perpetuate darkness and iniquity—to keep up a belief in what is utterly false and mischievous.

But there is a sort of common ground, neither Christian nor Hindoo, upon which the Hindoos often meet the missionary. Accepting his representations of God's natural attributes, and even of His moral nature as we understand it, they yet ply him with this illustration from dolls and toys. Now, I do not remember seeing the argument, when advanced under such circumstances, dealt with, as I should deal with it. I would meet it in some such way as the following : Our *dolls* are ladies and gentlemen *in miniature.* They are little inanimate *babies,* which the maternal instinct of the girl, though yet existing only in germ, loves to regard as living infants. And all the mimetic nature of the child is aroused in creating fanciful surroundings, such as a little cradle, for its artificial baby. Similarly the toys of boys, such as a rocking-horse, or a Noah's ark, or a plaything sword and gun—are miniature representations of *real life.* The basis of all is *resemblance.* By the *likeness borne by their toys to things living,* the children learn life and live it in anticipation. But where is the *likeness* between the hideous images which the Hindoos worship, and Him Who is the centre of moral beauty, and the Source of all natural loveliness? Where is the *resemblance* between the licentious Krishna, the blood-thirsty Kali, the idiotic figure of Juggurnath, and Him who is of "purer eyes than to behold evil."

It is here that the argument from dolls and toys in its application to idolatry entirely fails—*viz.,* in its utter incapacity to suggest by *resemblance* the character and attributes of God. Not a ray of light divine can emerge from the "gorgons and hydras and chimeras dire," which fill the idol temples—not a ray which can be said to emanate from the Fountain of purity and excellence.

COSMO.*

Statesman, September 25, 1882.

---

* NOTE.—This Letter was the first that was called forth by my discussion. It is no doubt the production of an educated and earnest English Christian, and it formed a welcome and encouraging contribution to the subject.—These Letters are all carefully reproduced with their own headings and signatures. W. H.

## II.—HASTIE *vs.* SRADHA.

To the Editor.

Sir,—Variety in nature is its beauty ; it is therefore no wonder that Mr. Hastie should pour out his feelings against the *élite* of the Hindoo community. Mr. Hastie is no doubt a man of much ability among his countrymen, and has no doubt sacrificed much for India ; he cannot, therefore, but be an object of compassion in the eyes of our Arya Dharma. Christians may pour out volumes of rhetorical writings and their logical reasons to inveigh our religion, but they cannot touch an iota of truth embodied in the bosom of Hindoo Shastras. Foreigners may say what they like of our religion ; but they are all looked with charity by those of us who have known the principles of our Arya Dharma. It is no delusion, it is as real as I hold my pen ; but to realise its truth, the whole of Western civilised learning is insignificant. A man must have practical training in its doctrine to realise his religious life. It may sound well in the mouths of missionary gentlemen to hear that the 'rising sun of knowledge dispels the nightmare of the dreamers.' But what is that knowledge that saves us from this 'world of shadows' ? Has Mr. Hastie realised that knowledge ? He is practically lying under the same delusions of which he complains. Is it not a fact that Christian missionaries have propensities and feelings in common with their lay brethren ? But a Hindoo devotee is taught to demolish his passions and desires and live in God alone. Religion is no theory to a Hindoo,—it is practical. Christianity may teach morality, but religion is ours ; and if Mr. Hastie wants to know further, he should bow down to his "Son of Man," with a simple and child-like heart and ask questions as these—Why one rose is red and another white ?—Why tigers do not live like lambs ? Why fire burns his hand ? in order to solve his difficulties.

OCKHOY CHUNDER KURMOKAR. *

Calcutta, September 23, 1882.

---

* Note.—This Correspondent is evidently a sincere and devoted Hindu. His theories that Religion is practical to the Hindu, that morality is proper to Christianity, and that the existing religious differences are ultimate, are characteristic of his standpoint. Although defective in English, his next letter shews him to be a Sanskrit Scholar. W. H.

## III.—Mr. HASTIE ON HINDOO IDOLATRY.

### To the Editor.

Sir,—Having perused Mr. Hastie's letters, finding fault with the indisposition of the enlightened Hindoos to abandon the idolatrous practices of their forefathers, and having read his remarks touching the idols of the Hindoos, I have been induced to make such observations in connection with them as naturally come into my mind. The intelligent Hindoos stick to these practices, as has been said on many occasions, not from any intrinsic regard for them. They do so, simply because they do not like to hurry themselves or to wound the feelings of their relations and countrymen, by publicly abandoning and despising the objects of their worship, while they do not find something that will be more acceptable to them than these idols. It is true that the high-born and intelligent Bengalee is not of a lower order of intelligence than either the *Karen*, the *Kol*, or some other similar tribe. Still, it is found that the latter are capable of appreciating the purest mode of worship, pointed out to them by the foreign missionaries, whereas the Bengali and other civilised Hindoos have proved to the missionaries so dull and dilatory about this matter. Again history shows that the very uncivilized nations of Europe were the first and the readiest converts to Christianity, more so than the civilized Greeks and Romans. This seemingly curious phenomenon, I think, will be explained by proceeding this way, namely :—

That man, in the primitive state of society, from the restlessness of his disposition. is unable patiently to examine into the justness and real worth of a thing. Prepossessed by the outward appearance of things, and interested by the advantages directly to be derived from them, he is either unable or unwilling to ponder for a moment over the future. From these circumstances, added to his native simplicity, he is placed in a favourable situation to allow any changes in his society, provided they prove to be gainsome to him. The case is quite different in a civilized community. Certainly the civilized man had been promoted to his present state under similar circumstances, but since that time he has had made great steps in the regions of thought and reasoning, so that now he cannot admit anything with his former precipitation. Such had been the case with the nations of Europe, and such undoubtedly is the case with the nations in India, where the Christian missionary converts the uneducated and simple-minded *Karen* and *Kol* with greater ease than he would the Bengali and other Hindoos. These, being placed in an age when civilization makes rapid strides, and improvements are being made daily in almost every sphere of human knowledge, are of course in search after truth, and if that truth be proved to be lodged in Christianity, they must some day receive it in their bosom.

Idolatry has so firm a footing in the popular Hindoo mind that, notwithstanding many members of the community are loath to yield a place for it in their mind, it cannot be easily removed from the society. Mankind must have some objects for his worship. The majority cannot think for themselves, and are very apt to be influenced by superior minds. So it seems to be in the primitive age in India ; the heads of certain tribes, or some intelligent men among them, conceived the figures and attributes of the Creator in various curious ways, and accordingly communicated their conceptions to those inferior to them, who in their turn gave suitable material forms to the Creator, and worshipped them. In this way idols multiplied according to the varied conceptions of different tribes. In some cases, perhaps, they borrowed from the high metaphysical conceptions of the Aryans who, most intent on determining the essence and attributes of the Creator, of himself, and everything around him, I say, who, in the process of the development of his philosophical reasonings, worshipped Him under various images. But so sublime is the Being, that at last His creatures could not compass Him by the limited range of their thought. Their efforts, however, gave rise to a class of philosophers, who see the world, the universe, filled with nothing other than dreams and delusions. These are recorded in the Shastras. Our Vedic forefathers probably, either being engrossed by these pursuits, had no time to communicate the results of their thoughts to the public, or did not like to puzzle the popular mind with those things which they thought to have been still imperfect. The ignorant people, on the other hand, enquiring for no other than what had been suggested to them, remained satisfied with them ; manufactured images after that suggestion, worshipped them, and latterly degeneracy was so great that they concentrated the whole idea of godhead in these images, which, being preserved, obtained the title of family deity from posterity. So flexible had been, indeed, the mind of our forefathers, that they did not hesitate to deify heroes and enterprizing men, whose images they worshipped, just like the idols abovementioned.

It is a very brilliant idea to imbue the Hindoo mind with "something more permanent and independent than these idols;" but it is not an easy matter to dislodge it from the attractive influence of these idols. Nor do the majority of the intelligent Hindoos find sufficient reason to neglect the teachings and religious principles of the Shastras, and accept those of the Bible, which they consider as interspersed with various improbabilities. If they are to accept these, they are at a loss to make out why they should abandon those which they already have separate from the Idolatry.

With due regard to the Christian missionary for his labour and trouble in trying to import into the country what he regards as the light of heaven, the intelligent and thinking Hindoo offers him every opportunity for his action, and lets him know that such is the state of the mind of his countrymen, from the agitation continually going on about matters of religion around him, that if he be satisfactorily convinced of its truest form in one, within one generation or so, the rising generation of the community will set in embracing it by hundreds and thousands. The land is open for the action of every minister of truth, and if they can give effectual aid to the inquiring mind here, they will find to their own satisfaction and to the well-being of the country, darkness dispelled from the face of it; otherwise, their work will continue to be very slow, and more rapid only in these cases where the temptation of of direct social advantage and comfort is predominant over that of being sheltered in the light of truth.

HARI CHARAN MUKERJI.*

**Calcutta, September 25, 1882.**

---

* NOTE.—Hari Charan Mukerji is a fair specimen of the large class of educated and semi-emancipated Hindus who satisfy themselves with superficial *pragmatic* reasoning about the practical

## IV.—Mr. HASTIE ON IDOLATRY.

### To the Editor.

Sir,—To do justice to both sides of a question, I beg that you may be good enough to insert the following in a corner of your paper.

Mr. Hastie's letter on idolatry, published in your Saturday's paper, has sadly disappointed us. We Hindus, had a great respect for a missionary like Mr. Hastie, who, we are told, gave up much better prospect of advancement in his own country for the sake of doing good to the people of Bengal. We accordingly expected to find in him a second Rev. Long, doing battle manfully for the weak and the oppressed, against the strong and the powerful, though they be of his own race. We say our expectations have been sadly disappointed, inasmuch as bigotry has never been known to produce any appreciable good, and Mr. Hastie may be fairly charged with it, as the occasion which produced his letter did not call for a display of his Christianity. On such an occasion, he might have pointed out the uselessness of spending thousands for feeding a certain number of men who are in no way benefited by the act, &c. ; but how idolatry became his theme on an occasion of a funeral ceremony passes our comprehension. *Gopinathjee* had been in the Raja's house long before the ceremony of *Shradh* took place. This then could not have called forth his eloquence. We believe, therefore, that he

---

evils of the past and the probable tendencies of the present. Undoubtedly the chief obstacle to the progress of Christianity in India is its peculiar semi-civilisation and especially its barbarism of Caste. But unfortunately, nothing could be farther from the truth than the closing paragraph. So far from the social despotism of the Hindus being abolished so that "the Hindoo offers the Christian missionary every opportunity for his action etc." Hari Babu knows very well that the "twice-born" Mukerjis would rise in a body and drive him out to starve without the least compunction, if he practically embraced Christianity. No doubt the victory will come, but it will be the lasting disgrace of this generation of Hindus that, with all their boasted Enlightenment, they resisted it at every step. I have had melancholy experience of this among the Mukerjis already. I hope to review the whole subject when I find leisure for a discussion of *the relation of Christianity to Social Reform in India.* W. H.

read this lecture to the Hindus, through your paper, thinking perhaps that he was not doing his duty as a missionary if he merely taught philosophy to the boys who attend his college. We never intended to discuss religious questions as they give rise to contention only. But since Mr. Hastie has thought fit to avail of any opportunity to express dislike to idolatry, we cannot refrain in this instance at least from expressing our views of Christianity as compared with idolatry, that he so strongly condemns, though we hope it will not be in so charitable a spirit as Mr. Hastie's.

*First.* As to the morality taught by the Gospels. We venture to affirm that there is not a single doctrine in the Bible which is not to be found in our *Shastras*, and that there are many more of equal value in our *Shastras* which are not to be found in the Bible. On this point we are prepared to go into details, if Mr. Hastie would have us to do so.

*Secondly.* As to the idea of God. In this also we are not so very far from the Christians, as Mr. Hastie seems to think. We willingly pass over the Catholic rite of transubstantiation and saint worship, as Mr. Hastie does not belong to that denomination of Christianity. His, *i. e.*, the Protestant notion of God, is, if we understand rightly, a Being or Intelligence in whom the good attributes of man carried to extremes are inherent, excluding of course the bad. Mr. Hastie is a philosopher ; it is therefore unnecessary to show that this notion itself contains a glaring absurdity. Nevertheless he would cling to it with all his might, till he falls upon faith as his last resource. Now he must admit that he tries to define the Unknowable, to give Him a shape, and that his definition does not stand the test of reason. The idolater knows as well that his theory also is untenable ; still by faith he gives shape to the Unknown, having no experience of spirit existing apart from matter. He makes his image, with this difference, that whereas he makes it tangible and definite, the Protestant makes it intangible and indefinite. It might, for aught we know, be a centaur or anything else compounded of mind and matter. The conception of Man-God is in both systems essentially the same.

As to the effects of Christianity on those who have embraced it, it has certainly made the ferocious Northmen sociable and polite, but has it made them humble ? No men are so proud as the Europeans. Has it made them turn their left cheek when their right is smitten ? No people are more aggressive. Christian charity is a theme of every missionary and Christian. What has it done ? It has depopulated the new world of its aboriginal inhabitants. It has subjugated independent nations. It has degraded the status of the nations it has visited. Death and destruction are in its train. Add to this, it has always a tendency to intolerance which is repressed only by the anti-Christian spirit now prevailing. We, however, do not believe that these are the legitimate effects of Christianity or Christian charity. We believe that a true Christian is as good a man and has as much chance of salvation as a true Hindu. We idolaters, however, have never been so intolerant as to consign every infidel to the Hell of the Protestants (which is worse than that of the Catholics, their Purgatory admitting hope), a creation which does credit to the Protestant imagination and to his Christian charity.

So much for Christianity. If the Hindus ever made any progress in any department of human knowledge, it was in religion, and Mr. Hastie's lecture to them on this subject is like the child on the shoulders of his father exclaiming with glee, " How much taller I am than papa." Mr. Hastie, however, is not satisfied with simply lecturing about the excellence of Christianity ; he must use hard terms against the Hindu idolaters. The Hindu idolaters are below savages, for many savages have given up idolatry, having embraced the Christian religion. Mr. Hastie should remember that not many hundred years ago, the people of Great Britain were not over-much civilised, living as they did in caves and hollows of trees. For him to say of a people whose civilisation dates as far back as the creation, and whose religious progress was immeasurable—for him, we say, to cast the word savage against them, is, to say the least, ridiculous.

In conclusion, we venture to think that it is absolutely bad taste to express one's hatred towards objects thought as sacred and held in veneration by another. If anything is wrong or pernicious in so thinking, it can be pointed out without calling names. Besides, religion is now pretty universally felt to be a personal or individual concern ; any interference in this matter is therefore quite unjustifiable.

Instead of rousing angry feelings, let us behave towards each other like brethren, and try to alleviate each other's sorrows in this vale of misery.

A BRAHMIN.*

Statesman, September 27, 1882.

---

## V.—HINDOO DOCTRINES.

### To the Editor.

Sir,—In to-day's *Statesman*, a correspondent, signing himself A Brahmin, writes : " We venture to affirm that there is not a single doctrine in the Bible, which is not to be found in our Shastras." It is easy to *affirm* ; it may not be so easy to *prove*. Pundit Nehemiah Goreh has been for years challenging all the Brahmins of India to produce any texts from their Shastras, asserting that the Supreme Being has ever *created* anything, or asserting that in our modern sense of the words, He is *holy*, or *just*, or that He *loves* men. Here are four Bible or Christian doctrines—(1) God is the Creator ; (2) God is holy ; (3) God is just ; (4) God loves men. Let a Brahmin take up the Christian pundit's challenge on any one of these four doctrines, and prove his point, and he will confer glory on himself and shut the mouth of the reviler of Hindooism, but lover of his Hindoo countrymen. I have repeated this challenge to scores upon scores of educated Hindoos, including learned pundits, but I have not found one yet who has taken it up, and answered it. Let A Brahmin take up one. Let him choose which he prefers ; and

---

* Note—The assertions of this remarkable Brahmin regarding the Brahmanical doctrines are well met by the Letter which follows. It is a too common mistake to suppose that "the conception of Man-God" in Hinduism is "essentially the same" as the doctrine of the "God-Man" in Christianity. The allegation that "Christian Charity, has depopulated the new world etc," would be parallelled by affirming that Hinduism has been the cause of Cholera (which indeed is much more reasonable) and of the ravages of Cyclones. It is charitable to admit that "a true Christian is as good a man, and has as much chance of salvation as a true Hindu"—O sancta Simplicitas !—but this charity as well as the mild liberalism of the last paragraph. is directly opposed to all the principles and traditions of the genuine "Brahmin." W. H.

stick to that one. But let him be sure that he understands his own quotations, and more especially the words on which the strength or weakness of his position depends.

In his book, *Theism and Christianity*, published at the Oxford Mission Press, the learned Christian pundit not only challenges the pundits of India to produce the missing texts, but he himself produces a number of Sanskrit texts in the original and in translation, denying the truth of every one of these four Christian doctrines, and I have met pundits who have taken up that position, but not the opposite. If A BRAHMAN succeeds in proving what he has affirmed, he will, in doing that, also prove that the Hindoo Shastras flatly contradict themselves.

By-the-bye, Mr. Editor, would you kindly explain to me what is meant by saying that Dr. Rajendra Lala Mitra is a *shevait*, and conducts the *sheva* of the idol ?

A STUDENT OF HINDOOISM.*

September 28, 1882.

---

## VI.—MR. HASTIE AND IDOLATRY.

### TO THE EDITOR.

Sir,—Regarding the strictures made by the Rev. W. Hastie, " on the idolatrous Hindoo religion for paying divine honor to the family idol *Gopeenathjee*, on the occasion of the late Sobha Bazaar Rajbaree *shradh*, allow me to quote two paras from a letter of Mr. A. O. Hume, re-

---

* NOTE—This Challenge, no doubt from a Christian, was quite relevant, straight-forward and fair. It remained unnoticed, however. The reference to Dr. Rajendra Lala Mitra was pungent and well timed. This distinguished Scholar had been elected for years as a Member of the Calcutta Municipal Body, but his right to represent the Ratepayers was publicly questioned by some of his Hindu rivals on the ground that he was not himself a Ratepayer. The case was referred to the High Court when it was found that Dr. Mitra's claim to the full rights of Citizenship rested upon his presiding over the idolatrous rites and property of the family Idol ! The claim was very properly disallowed by the High Court, and Dr. Mitra's election was declared void.

'Who would not laugh, if such a man there be ?
Who would not weep, if Atticus were he ?' W. H.

published in the *Theosophist* for September last from the Allahabad *Pioneer*, which I trust you will kindly publish in your valuable journal :

" It might as well be said that the people of Europe were an idolatrous nation, because the lower classes in Italy, Spain, Greece, Russia and Ireland do, in defiance of the teachings of their respective churches, *worship* images and pictures of Virgins, Saints, and Christ, only *intended* to serve as mementoes or *guides* to devotion. Truly the Hindu religion is far less idolatrous than that religion set forth by the great churches of Europe, and miscalled Christianity. In these the mass of their adherents distinctly acknowledge a belief in an anthropomorphic God, —a God that is angry : that repenteth himself ; that lives; in fact, only a magnified image in the sky of a good man. The worship of such a concrete conception of the Infinite is truly as much idolatry *in principle*, as the worship of the still lower and more concrete conception embodied in a statue."

" Of course the people of India believe, just as do the people of Europe, that between man and the Almighty there are many grades of intelligent beings. We call them Cherubim, and Seraphim, and Angels. The Indians have other names for them, but all the names refer to the same real existences. *Real!* Yes, my Christian friends, I notice the smile of contempt that curls your lips at this word. You have quite outgrown the superstition of angels and the like ! Still, they are none the less facts, and India is here much nearer the truth than you are !"

A HINDOO.

---

NOTE.—The Theosophists are the most conspicuous religious Charlatans of the time in India. It is difficult to believe that any one of them—even Madame Blavatzky the romantic Russian Princess, the modern Medea with the magic of unfading youth, or the mighty American colonel himself—can be in sober earnest. The most important thing said or done by Mr. Joseph Cook in India, was his practical exposure of this mythical and mystical party. It is extremely disappointing to find even a couple of Englishmen following in this train in loving companionship with a few educated Baboos who seem always ready to follow anything *but* the truth.

W. H.

## VII.—Mr. HASTIE AND IDOLATRY.

### To the Editor.

Sir,—It was not without considerable surprise that I perused the long letter from Mr. Hastie in your issue of the 26th instant, in which he attacks, in most violent terms, the religion of the Hindus. As Englishmen always boast of their love of fair play, I presume your columns will be equally open to articles attacking the Christian religion.

Missionaries appear to think that if the religion of the Hindus is done away with, then Christianity will be at once embraced by all. But when an educated man changes his religion, it is after careful study from all sides of the new creed. Now that we can all read Buckle, Huxley, Darwin, Paine, Ingersoll, Mill and such like, who talk with authority, the shallow arguments of the missionary fall flat, and until they are able to show some better reasons for the faith they profess, they cannot expect to make progress in converting any but the ignorant, or those who find it improves their financial prospects.

It would be very interesting to your Hindu readers if you would print some of, say, Ingersoll's lectures with Mr. Hastie's notes thereon attached.

FAIR PLAY.*

Calcutta, September 27, 1882.

---

## VIII.—Mr. HASTIE AND IDOLATRY.

### To the Editor.

Sir,—The letters of Mr. Hastie on idolatry, lately published in your journal, have taken a great many of the educated Hindus by surprise. First, because a *shrad*, or funeral ceremony, is certainly not a proper subject to give rise to theological controversy; and secondly, because

---

* Note.—"Fair Play"—if he be a Hindu and not an English secularist—could hardly find less 'fair' or more 'shallow' guides upon the religious question than his admired Ingersoll and Co. An opportunity may occur for discussing the religious value of scientific secularism again; meanwhile it may be said, that the Christian religion is afraid of no attacks from such men, but it is most lamentable to see "the religious Hindu" so completely victimised by them. "A little Knowledge is a dangerous thing." W. H.

Mr. Hastie is under the delusion that one or two letters of his, however well written, will convert the educated Hindus into Christianity. One who has carefully marked the present status of an educated Hindu, might safely affirm that he is no longer liable to be converted to Christianity or any kind of religion. As for Christian missionaries that are very desirous of making converts, not India, but Cape Colony or Madagascar is the place for them, as Mr. Hastie has very truly observed,that the savage tribes are more pliable than Hindus in their notion of God, because the savage man's notion of God can be very soon and easily moulded and shaped and converted by a Christian missionary, whereas a Hindu's notion of God is so firmly stamped in his mind that neither lectures nor sermons, nor street preachings, nor published letters can efface it. As for idolatry, it is bad if it usurps the throne of God Almighty, not if it is merely a symbol to enable man to reach that throne. The Christians send their offerings to God through Christ, the Mahomedans through Mahomed, the Hindus through Durga, Kali and others ; and the Brahmos through imaginary beings manufactured by themselves, in their minds. None can approach the unknown, unsearchable God, alone and without a director or something to direct them. Men must have something by which to worship the unknown God ; some employ symbols and others employ sounds. Lord, Almighty, Father, Mother, Saviour, Preserver, are sounds which some employ to give rise in their minds to certain earthly feelings or notions which they are pleased to attribute to God. Doorga, Kali, Brahma, Siva, are symbols which also give rise in the human mind to certain earthly feelings, which others are pleased to attribute to godhead. In many cases the very same series of feelings which arise on the utterance of a single sound also arise on the perception of a single symbol. The difference is that in one case the tongue or power of speech is put in motion, and in the other case the power of sight is exercised ; in one case there is an ideal manifestation in the mind of a Supreme Being, and in the other there is physical manifestation of the same Being. The one is as much man's creation as the other. The one is as much unlike the unknown God as the other. The one is as much of the earth, earthy, as the other. The one is as much insulting to God as the other. The one is as much idolatry as the other. If there is any distinction between the two, it is the same distinction which is found between a piece of thread and a common string. The one is thin and the other is thick, but both are strings, *i. e.*, made of the very same stuff. Controversy cannot change them, cannot make them better or more distinct. But controversy can do one thing at least, it can destroy both the strings. Therefore, let controversy cease.

NUNDOLAL DUTTA.*

Sulkea, September 30, 1882.

---

## IX.—Mr. HASTIE AND IDOLATRY.

To the Editor.

Sir,—Nowhere is diversity so perceptible as in the Hindu *shastras*, and none but disinterested, profound thinkers who have made it the principal subject of their study, can find harmony amid this immense diversity. Its own expositors, the Brahmans, have become degenerated, and look with apathy on the works of their forefathers ; it is therefore no wonder that that harmony should be imperceptible to a foreigner, who has been brought up in an altogether different atmosphere, and has not known it except from the interpretation of another man like himself. Unlike Christianity, Hinduism is vast, and it is not improbable that some interested men have alloyed it with principles which serve their own motives, but notwithstanding these insinuations, volumes may be written in proof of its harmony, but such labour is profitless, as the works themselves are replete with testimonies. The object of every instructor has been to elevate mortal man into the one immortal soul, and to attain this stage several ways have been prescribed. The

---

* Note.—This letter though written in clear English and in a pointed style, is however singularly illogical. The general position is agnostic, and yet the writer pronounces upon the true mode of worshipping, conceiving and symbolising God, confounds historical personalities with mythical fancies. asserts the necessity of a religion yet declares the Hindu incapable of rising above his own "earthy ideas and inventions," and demands the cessation of controversy by controversy. In view of *this* religious nihilism the devout Hindu, may well say, Non tali auxilio." W. H.

inculcations of *Tantras*, though seemingly at variance with those of the *Vaisnavas* have but one object, that of reconciling the human soul to its Maker. The so-called blood-thirsty *Kali* is said as a *Param Vaishnavi*, and has this no meaning ? Nay, I would point out that what the missionary calls the lustfulness in *Krishna*, is replete with religious teachings. The life of *Krishna* is simply to show the worldly man how he should behave himself though possessed of pleasures however great. He lived in the world with pleasures, but no amount of enjoyment could subdue him. Did he not instantly quit the *Brajangana* when duty called him away ? Did he merge himself in the *Rash* ? Far from it ; he quitted the place the moment his *Gopinis* thought themselves master over him ; and does not this clearly depict to the worldly man that he should be above the reach of worldly pleasures and vanities ? Read his precepts to *Arjuna*, to *Udhyaba* ; read *Bhagabata* entire, and then you shall see Krishna is not the Krishna as you now take him to be ; he is a model of perfection for a fallen man to rise. Sanskrit language cannot be grasped by an untutored mind, especially its ancient writings ; hence harmony is imperceptible to a superficial observer.

To show the world that Mr. Hastie understands the highest philosophy of the Hindus he has quoted certain passages, and then proceeds to remark that " first of all it is obvious to remark that negative ideas give no satisfactory explanation of the existence of the world and the stable order, and consequently gives no foundation for practical activities of life or the objective interest of modern science." Certainly, but has Mr. Hastie read such passages in the Hindu *shastras* as

> "Niyatam kuru karmmatam karmojaajhya akarmana
> Sareerajatrapicha tena prosidhetta karmana."

Again—

> "Jodijhaham nabartayam jatukarmanyatantrata
> Mamabartmanubartanta manusya parthasarbasa."

So you see neither the Hindu nor his god is inactive, but we must bear in mind that everything has its turn. Work you must, but what then ? is it not rest and peace ?

*Secondly.* Mr. Hastie goes on to say " again this theory indirectly gives no moral meaning or purpose to human life." Does the ultimate rest and peace give no moral meaning to human life? Is it so with Christianity? What do its followers expect in Heaven?

*Thirdly.* Mr. Hastie says "Brahminism again manifestly leaves its votary ultimately in the melancholy and despair of having no hope and without God in the world." Far from it. No system of religious precepts has attained that stage of perfection as that of the Hindus. Mortal man is grown into a spiritual man, and the all-pervading spirit is then visible to him. To perceive God in the animal nature of man is a dream, which can only be found in the modern science of Christian philosophy. But the Hindoo *shastras* enjoin to live without food, to demolish passions and all animal propensities, after a man has fulfilled his mission on earth; and then he should seek to approach the Almighty Perfect. Thus far need it be repeated that to rush into public print for reviling the doctrines inculcated in another's religion is degrading to missionaries in the native view of it, and it is quite incompatible with the character of Christ. If Christianity has any Purity superior to Hinduism, show it by your life and actions, and it will be brought home to us. But so long Mr. Hastie continues reviling we bid him good-bye.

OKHOY CHUNDER KURMOKAR.*

September 30, 1882.

---

## X.—THE SOBHA BAZAR RAJBAREE SHRADH.

To the Editor.

Sir,—We have read with thrilling interest the remarkable letters of Mr. W. Hastie, of the General Assembly's College (that appeared in your columns), embodying reflec-

* This second letter from this earnest Hindu contains the only attempt made to meet my criticism of the Brahmanical philosophy, and it will be taken at what it is worth. The truth is that the speculative genius of Hinduism expired long ago from mere intellectual Asphyxia. It could neither expire the deadening Carbonic of its own false abstractions, nor inspire the free healthgiving Oxygen of the surrounding air. Its *breathing* must be again restored for the sake of its *heart* and *brain*.—Nothing more, need be said of the thievish, lustful, indulgent Krishna, as a Divine Incarnation and Example. We know now how he attained to the preeminence and wisdom attributed to him in the Bhagavata. W. H.

tions on the conduct of men like Dr. Rajendralala Mitra, Sir Jotendra Mohun Tagore, and the Hon'ble Kristo Das Pal, as well as on the absurdities of Hindu idolatry in general. Had the learned Bachelor of Divinity been content to keep close to metaphysics alone, his unintelligibility might have secured for him a position of great vantage, for it is an almost universally acknowledged privilege of metaphysicians and philosophers to look down with contempt upon the existing order of things, and to give utterance to words and opinions (however unwelcome they might otherwise be) with perfect safety to their life and limbs. The dull matter-of-fact men of the world have the patience to observe the most provoking neutrality with regard to the particular opinions of this or that philosopher, so long as such opinions touch not their religious sensibilities. They can, for instance, tolerate a Darwin in spite of his monkeys and monkey-descended men, for the obvious reason that the great advocate of the monkey origin of man claims not for himself a pedigree more respectable than that of his fellow brethren. But the reception which the advocate of one particular sect or creed can expect to receive from men whom he would fain shut out from heaven is likely to be different. The obtrusively hasty preacher is instantly given to understand by his hearers—who, satisfied long ago with regard to the relative merits and demerits of the different systems of religion now extant in the world, persist nevertheless in conforming to the one professed by their forefathers—that his lecture is quite superfluous, and that his remarks on persons and things with which he has no concern are simply *impertinent.*

We fear Mr. Hastie has done the greatest injustice to himself by standing up as a champion of one class of exploded superstitions against another. The zeal of a missionary iconoclast, armed at a moment's notice with the battle-axe of personality, carries him, we are sorry to say, to a length which the more prudent among his own brethren would certainly have called *rashness.* For, just as our learned B. D. gratuitously assumes that intelligent Hindus have no faith in their idols and that they are conformists only from motives of policy, may we not as fairly contend that all the most intelligent converts to Christianity, as well as Christians of Mr. Hastie's learning and ability, have long given up the dogmas that a Virgin could conceive of the "Holy Ghost," or that God's fair world could be created in six days' time, or that the Confusion of Tongues could be brought about in the way in which the Bible tells us it was, as untenable ? Why need we multiply instances of such absurdities with which the works of the Hebrew prophets and Christian evangelists are replete ? The good old missionaries, who, attacked on their own ground, and with weapons they at one time wielded with telling effect against the Hindus, have long ago withdrawn themselves from the arena of religious disputation. It is no use flogging a dead horse, with regard to a method of attacking Hinduism which has often been weighed in the balance, and as often found wanting. As regards the charge of inconsistency to which men like Dr. Rajendra Lala Mitra, Sir Jotendro Mohun Tagore, the Hon'ble Kristo Das Pal, &c., are held liable by reason of their sanctioning idolatry with their presence, we think Mr. Hastie ought to have borne in mind that men,—intelligent men, like Father Lafont, Cardinal Newman, and our beloved ruler, the Marquis of Ripon, are all idolaters ; they have their pictures, images and relics, and if they themselves do not believe in them, they still belong to a sect of which idolatry itself is the most prominent feature. But that which surprises us most is the happy-go-lucky way in which Mr. Hastie has disposed of the famous argument of the late Raja Radhakant Deb on the necessity of tolerating idolatry as a religion to keep the mass in order. Mr. Hastie seems in his hurry to emulate the fame of St. Paul, and has been a little unhappy in the choice of his illustrations. He cites the case of the Mahomedans and the converted Kookies and Lepchas, who, however illiterate, not only discard idols, but can comprehend the abstract idea of a living God. Whether Mr. Hastie has run away with this notion by a superficial glance at the census returns or not, is not ours to say ; but it can be safely maintained that any man, far below Mr. Hastie in point of intellectual attainments, is perfectly aware of the dry fact, so often noticed by travellers, and complained of by missionaries, that savages, even when converted to Christianity, stick to the superstitions of their ancestors with a tenacity against which all arguments and remonstrances of missionaries are unavailing. Mr. Hastie will, we doubt not, himself admit that the Lepchas and Kols do not make such good Christians as he, for argument's sake, is inclined to believe. The way in which missionaries, in famine times especially, manage to baptise those savages, ought to cry shame to the zeal of those pious preachers of the Cross. The shortest way to the heart, says the proverb, is down the mouth ; and the missionaries by making the most of this simple proverb in times of scarcity, add, it is true, a considerable number of proselytes to the religion which they are paid to preach. But the question is—do these men continue to remain Christians after the famine time is over ? We pause for an answer. Let Mr. Hastie examine facts which will plead for themselves. No sooner is the famine time over, than out go needy Brahmins from the neighbouring districts, with their stocks and stones, to proselytise the aborigines of the Kol and Santhal countries ; and with what results ? Groves are consecrated, shapeless blocks of stones set up, and Kols and Dhangurs flock to the Hindu missionaries, who offer them visible and tangible gods in the place of a Man-God who died nineteen hundred years ago, in a country far away from their native jungles. The missionary work is thus at once undone ! !

As regards the Mahomedans of India, the lower class, of course,—are they really Mahomedans at all ? Let Mr. Hastie, with the patience of a missionary, be a little more careful in studying the habits of the lower class of Mahomedans in India, and he will at once be convinced of his error. Besides, what is the festival of *mohurrum* itself ? Is it not looked upon by one class of Mahomedans—by far the most intelligent of the two—as an idolatrous innovation on the strictly monotheistic teachings of the Koran ? The fact, in itself, is undeniable. In all countries and in all ages, even in the highest state of civilisation, people have felt the necessity of having an idol round which to shout their devotion. Witness the statue of the goddess of *Reason* and the tree of *Liberty* that made so much noise a century ago in France. Even the Jews, whose frequent relapse to idolatry is noticed by Gibbon, and at a time when miracles were as rife as blackberries, had an idol in the Ark of the covenant in their Sukhania, even in days when by long education they had altogether abjured idolatries. The Mahomedans, too, have their *kaaba* and their Mecca—some tangible, visible symbol wherewith to grasp the Invisible and the Incomprehensible. How far metaphysicians are at one with regard to this necessity in human nature, we leave Mr. Hastie to determine. Suffice it for our purpose to say, that that great anti-Hindu movement, fraught with such incalculable blessings to humanity at large, the celebrated religion of Sakya Sinha, dealing as it did with pure abstractions, found, precisely for the reasons stated above, no permanent hold upon the millions of India. It flourishes, indeed, in countries outside India, the land of its origin, just as Christianity flourishes in Europe, and not in Palestine. But is the ancestor and relic-worshipping Chinese or the Lama-worshipping Thibetan, the true follower of the prince of Kapilavyasta, or is the Irish pilgrim kissing his holy father's toe the follower of that Jesus of Nazareth who thundered damnation on all that sought any other way to the Kingdom of His Father than His Anointed Son ? Mr. Hastie might have done well to study the past history of missionary labor in India from the time of St. Francis Xavier down to his own, he might then have seen how ably were the gods and goddesses of the Hindus assailed by his predecessors ; how he was anticipated (perhaps 50 years before he was born) in his arguments against idolatry by missionaries like Dr. Marshman and Dr. Duff, and the whole host of fanatical catechists ; he might then have seen that as many times as it was pointed out by Christian *Padrees* that Hinduism was full of errors and inconsistencies and obscenities, so many times was the charge retorted upon and ably substantiated against that Book of books—the Hebrew Bible ; he might then have seen that the monstrosities of the Hebrew Jehova are almost at par with those laid at the door of some of the Hindu gods and goddesses ; he might then have seen that, in order to reclaim the benighted Hindus, the Christian missionaries were required to show better cause why one system of absurdities should have preference over another. So that we cannot help thinking Mr. Hastie, as a discoverer, has come too late with his discoveries. Moreover, Mr. Hastie is very indignant to see Dr. Rajendralala Mitra, Sir Jotendra Mohun Tagore, and Hon'ble Kristo Das Pal to be inconsistent, but we are in no way prepared to sympathise with him : for if it can be shown that all men from Solomon down to W. Hastie are alike open to the charge of being inconsistent in more serious particulars—this ami-

K

able inconsistency on the part of those ornaments of our society ought, we hope, to be viewed by Mr. Hastie with some few grains of allowances.

Whether idolatry is synonymous with, or worse than, atheism, is a question we leave to such learned theologians as Mr. Hastie himself to determine. He may quote Hume and Bacon whenever it serves his turn to expose the absurdities of pantheistic systems of religion, and never allude to the famous essay on miracle as something foreign to his purpose ; and with due deference to the opinions of so learned a man as Mr. Hastie, we beg to assure him that his good words anent idolatry have fallen on the wayside, only to be devoured up by the fowls of the air.

An odd idea strikes our man of God at the sight of so much pomp and magnificence, and the temptation for drawing a parallel seems too irresistible to him ; he tells us with much pathos how a modern St. Paul (no other than himself) would address the benighted heathens of Calcutta. But there is a temptation *equally* strong on our part for drawing a parallel which we trust the learned Bachelor of Divinity will be charitable enough to excuse ; we would, for instance, fancy the whole *Shradha* ceremony to be as grand an affair as the installation of Gadisthira after the battle of Kivinksetra ; we would imagine the famous men to whose presence at the occasion Mr. Hastie takes particular exception to be the heroes that survived that fatal war ; we would suppose the obscure class of feasters to be the *mobilus vulgus* that might have attended at the ceremony to swell the shout of *vive le roi*, and we should, in order to make the parallel more complete, liken the learned pundits with Mr. Hastie sitting amongst them in the disguise of a Brahmin, to be the Brahmins and Pundits that must have graced the ceremony with their presence; then we must suppose our disguised Brahmin—Mr. Hastie, to be up on his legs, the observed of all observers. The whole gathering is hushed in silence, and our over hasty speaker begins to pour volleys of abuses upon the Pandavas and their allies. The hearers are not long in finding out who the unwelcome speaker is ; he is instantly known to be an enemy of the friend of Durjodhan,—the Raksasa Charbak, not certainly a blood-thirsty cannibal, but a thinker much in advance of his age, and then—oh ! the uproar of the people at his detection.—" Down with the wretch" resounds from every quarter of the gathering, and in spite of the efforts of those whom he most abused, and who would spare his life if they could, our too hasty and indiscreet philosopher, whose only fault is that he could not keep his own counsel till some better opportunity, is hacked to pieces by the infuriated mob.

**A CONSTANT READER.***

**Motihari, September 29, 1882.**

---

## XI.—HINDUISM *vs.* MR. HASTIE.

### TO THE EDITOR.

SIR,—Variety is the law of nature. There is necessarily as much variety in religion as there is in human character. To expect otherwise, is to expect an impossibility. The whole history of mankind shows us that the tendency of religion is to split up into sectarianism sooner or later. Christianity with its Nestorian, Manichean, Optimist, and Armenian heresies ; even Christian Protestantism with its sub-sects, the Baptists, the Unitarians, and in addition the Quakers ; Mahomedanism with its Sufism, its Haniffee and sixty other sects, and Hinduism with its Sivaite, Vishnaivite and other divisions ; why, even Brahmoism, in its new-fangled form, with its Adi, Kesavite, and Sadharan branches, prove that the tendency of religion, instead of being towards union, is in the contrary direction. Dr. Johnson used to say that no two sane men can have the same religion. Why should Mr. Hastie or anybody else fret over the diversity in the religious tenets of different nations ? It is, in our humble opinion, barely impossible for such variety to exist, nay, to multiply, unless it be the Divine intention that it should be so. Doctrinal differences as to the nature of God must exist for ever. Such differences are, however, immaterial. If God be, as we all believe, able to understand our hearts, I do not understand why He will not accept my worship offered

---

* To obviate further delay the earlier copies will be printed from this point, without the intended foot-notes, but they will be inserted in the later copies. **W. H.**

with a sincere heart and accept yours. Supposing, for the sake of argument, that your notion of the Godhead is more correct than mine, and yet my devotion is not a whit inferior to yours, will not God be pleased with my honest faith and my heartfelt prayer? I have no faith in a jealous God, angry God, a God who loves you more than He loves me, because I am not equally wise, or rather equally intelligent. I know that God is the Supreme Intelligence, that he is Omniscient, and therefore knows our hearts, and that He is All-Merciful, and therefore he can take no offence, if I am mistaken. It is no wonder that we can have no clear conception of God. He is Infinite and Eternal; so is He incomprehensible. Therefore all attempts to understand Him must necessarily be useless. So far as our capacity reaches, we think or meditate on him, so we cannot be guilty. St. Paul spoke of the law in the mind of man which should guide him. If he follows that law he will sit with Abraham and Isaac in heaven. Mr. Hastie can have nothing to say against this, I suppose. Indeed, the mere formalities of religion, even the more or less correct idea of the Godhead cannot materially affect our relation to Him. Suppose you have a more intelligent notion of the Supreme Being, you cannot on that account be saved. A Christian highwayman cannot necessarily be transported to the seventh heaven after death, and a pious and truly good Hindoo hurled headlong to the lowest depths of perdition. No, we judge of a tree by its fruits. Moral conduct, true heartfelt devotion to God, are at least as much to be met with among Hindus as among Christians. Philosophical discussions cannot, and do not, influence our conduct. Nations that go to war on the slightest provocation, nations that feel no compunction in shedding human blood and inflicting misery upon thousands of their fellow creatures, with Egypt, Zululand, Algiers, Turkey or Afghanistan reeking with carnage, whose bloody banners have been unfurled in every age and clime, have no right to call in question the morality, that is to say, the religion, of the Hindus. True morality is true religion. "God sees the heart. He judges by the will." As to esoteric religion, Christianity, as well as Hinduism, has thrown philosophy overboard. In fact, revelation, notwithstanding Paley and Butler, cannot be very nicely reconciled with philosophy, so Mr. Hastie should leave the philosophical analysis of Hinduism, as also of his own religion, an open question.

Hindu mythology affords an ample ground of attack. And yet it is not unique in the history of religion. Christianity with its whole host of seraphs and cherubs, its Michael, Gabriel and Ariel, with Satan and Beelzebub tracing a family resemblance to the followers of Ahurmazda and Ahriman, Judaism its mother, and Mahomedanism its sister, with an equal number of gods, have nothing to say against the Hindu pantheon ; the numbers may vary, but they agree as to the principle. It is beyond human ability to understand what machinery God employs in the government of the world, or whether He employs any machinery at all. So far as we now understand, all our ideas regarding God and His actions have been borrowed from man, and thus far our idea of the Creator is created. We cannot help it. As to the veracity of the Hindu mythology, we fear that one who puts his faith upon the stories of Moses' rod, the Egyptian sorcerers, the standing still of the sun at Gibeon, of Jonah, of Elijah, and the thousand-and-one miracles recorded in the Bible has no right to call our faith in question. Mr. Hastie should think twice before he cites Hume again to demolish the Hindu religion, for he knows how Hume has dealt with his own. In short, for aught we know, there is as much want of proof, ocular or tangible, of the existence of the Hindu gods as of the Judaic or Zoroastrian angels. It is waste of valuable time to discuss what machinery the Lord of Creation employs. It stands to reason with equal force that He may make use of inferior gods in the government of the universe or He may not. Who are we to inquire about such things ? Idolatry is another bugbear. Carlyle may laugh at the white European who has his offensive idols at home, but who looks down with contempt on the black African's Mumbo Jumbo. But they are different idols. I would refer Mr. Hastie to the remark of the Benares pundit given in the preface to Max Müller's *Chips from a German Workshop*. Professor Max Müller calls Hinduism a Kathenotheism, not as Mr. Hastie would have it. It is not exactly pantheistic, though for the matter of that, there are as many pantheists among Christians as among Hindus. The image of God is unreasonable we all admit, but Hinduism does *not* make an image of the God, but of minor gods.

What has Mr. Hastie to say when the Bible says, "In the image of God made He him?" The image may be ideal, mental if you like, still it is an image. When God appeared to Moses in the wilderness and said, "I am what I am;" or when He appeared to James and said, "This is my beloved Son," have you then no conception of some Being who speaks like a human being? Does not speech imply a tongue and a mouth? Does not light imply colour? Wherein does then the Hindu err more than Christians? However pure or high our notions of God may be, we must fall short of the original. All human efforts in that direction are vain, and we must learn to be content with the light He has vouchsafed to us.

QUIXOTE SENIOR.

---

## XII. THE MODERN ST. PAUL.

To the Editor.

Sir,—Will you allow me to suggest to Mr. Hastie, who is so ambitious of earning distinction as a sort of Indian St. Paul, that it is fit that he should render himself better acquainted with the doctrines of the Hindoo religion before he seeks to demolish them? As matters stand with him, his arguments are simply contemptible; and I think the columns of the *Statesman* might have been more usefully occupied by advertisements about Doorga Pooja holiday goods than by trash which renders the champion of Christianity contemptible in the eyes of idolaters. This may be harsh language, but the writer who mistakes Vedantism, for Hindooism, and goes to Mr. Monier Williams for an exposition of that doctrine, hardly deserves better treatment. Mr Hastie's attempt to storm "the inner citadel" of the Hindoo religion forcibly reminds us of another equally heroic achievement—that of the redoubted knight of La Mancha before the windmill.

Let Mr. Hastie take my advice, and obtain some knowledge of Sanskrit scriptures in the original. Let him study then critically all the systems of Hindoo philosophy—the *Bhagabat-gita*, the *Bhakti Suka* of Sandilya, and such other works. Let him not study them under European scholars, for they cannot teach what they don't understand;

the blind cannot lead the blind. Let him study them with a Hindoo, with one who *believes* in them. And then, if he should still entertain his present inclination to enter on an apostolic career, let him hold forth at his pleasure, and if we do not promise to be convinced by him, we promise not to laugh at him. At present, arguments would be thrown away on him. There can be no controversy on a subject when one of the controversialists is in utter ignorance on the subject-matter of the controversy ; and if under such circumstances the "Olympians only yawn," and do not assert, Mr. Hastie has only to thank his own precipitate ignorance.

RAM CHANDRA.

*Statesman*, October 6, 1882.

---

## XIII. THE MODERN RAM CHANDRA.

### To the Editor.

Sir,—I do not intend to ask space for a reply to any of the *special* criticisms of your numerous correspondents upon my letters, until they say something relevant and worthy of being dealt with. But I hope you will allow me to return my grateful thanks to the valiant hero of the modern Brahmans, Ram Chandra *Redivivus*, for the kind advice so bountifully tendered to me in your columns today, which I sincerely promise to put into practice, as soon as he shows that I have need of it. Your readers, who may be better acquainted with Sanskrit literature than he seems to be, will have already judged whether I confounded Vedantism with Hinduism, or whether I did not rather most rigidly distinguish them in my discussion. I have certainly not committed the obvious blunder of ranking the "Bhagabat-gita and Bhakti Suka of Sandilya" ( did he write *Suka ?* ) among the "systems of Hindu philosophy," although as these religious reflections are now most completely open to the European student, I gladly recognise them as the pearls of Sanskrit literature ; and as I stated in some letters on Krishna a year ago, I am forced to follow the European Sanskritists who hold that their exceptional spirituality can only be explained from their having originated directly or indirectly, under a Christian influence.

But however unworthy my own views may be of consideration, I must again protest against this treatment of the great Sanskrit scholars of Europe who have brought all the riches and depths of the ancient Aryan literature within universal appropriation and enjoyment This *dodge* of turning round the corner, when forced to an extremity by fair argument and disappearing *a posteriori* in subterranean darkness, will no longer avail the Hindu apologists. I assert, with a confidence grounded on the judgment of all competent critics, that both the Sanskrit language and the Sanskrit literature are much better understood at this moment in Europe and America than they are in India, and that native pundits, like RAM CHANDRA, are quite helpless against the logical inferences deducible from this knowledge of them. A man may live all his days in the thick of a wood and never be able to see it for the trees ; whereas the adventurous traveller, who comes upon it unexpectedly, may take in its outline and bearings at a glance, may rapidly traverse it through and through, and then instruct us with a thoroughly scientific account of all its elements and growths. Such, indeed, is the relation of the native Sanskrit verbalist, with his merely mechanical memory for phrases, to the scientific European scholar whose intellectual superiority is beyond all question, and so beneficent that its claims should surely now be gratefully recognised even by the benighted successors of the ancient Rishis.

When Max Müller undertook to edit and explain the Vedas, the pundits of Bengal declared that the thing was *impossible*, and that even a complete copy of them could not be had for love or money. The word " impossible " does not bulk so largely in the vocabulary of the European as of the Hindu, and we know how the accomplished German scholar has fulfilled his task. But when an occasional perplexity arose, as it will with the best, it was not to the native commentator or pundit that he turned for final aid, but to European scientists of an entirely different order and tendency. Let me take one of these as a practical test of the *right* of this supercilious and self-confident RAM CHANDRA to *write* upon the *rites* of the Hindoo religion as he has done. I publicly challenge him to substantiate his allegation of the " contemptible" inferiority of " blind" European learning by giving, without its aid, an intelligible explanation of the simple

Vedic verse—"Chatustrinsadvajino devabandhorvankri-rasvasya svadhitih sameti"—as in the ORIGINAL.* I give him the whole of the Durga Puja holidays even to discover the difficulty involved in the expression, and if he does find out so much, I will give him, and the other 4,000 *Adyapaks* to boot, who were present at the great *Shradh* as many months as they like, to search through all the Sanskrit literature known to them, for, an explanation. And if, at last, they all give it up, as they did the editing of the Vedas, I shall then give them the luminous convincing solution of the problem, discovered, after it had been forgotten for about 3,000 years, by a European who, so far as I know, is not even acquainted with the letters in which this divinest literature of the Ram Chandras is written.

This seems a much more definite and practical method of dealing with the question of competency, than the vague vituperation of your contemptuous correspondent; and should he succeed in solving this simple Sanskrit problem, and write under his own honest patronymic, I shall then supply him as a reward for his cleverness, with a few harder ones out of a plentiful fund in store,—if only to keep up his happy flow of laughter, and prevent him from subsiding again into the Olympian yawn.

W. HASTIE.

The General Assembly's Institution,
October 6, 1882.

---

## XIV.—THE CHALLENGE RENEWED.

### To the Editor.

Sir,—Although you have twice declined to insert my closing letter on the subject of the Hindu idolatry, I hope you will allow me to state, that, in accordance with the suggestion of friends in the Church of Scotland Mission, it is being printed along with the other five which have appeared in your columns, and for the insertion of

* चतुस्त्रिंशद्वाजिनो देवबंधोर्वंक्रीरश्वस्य स्वधितिः समेति ।

which I would publicly thank you. I shall be glad to supply copies *gratis* to Hindu students if they will apply for them, after Tuesday, at the General Assembly's Institution, or to any others who may have been interested in this discussion, and especially to Missionaries engaged in work among the educated natives, if they would be of any use to them.

I also beg to state that I *may* reprint the other letters which have appeared in your columns on the subject, as an illustrative appendix to mine, unless the writers inform me that they object to this being done. My only reason for doing so, is to give the other side a fair hearing.

I shall only add that I am waiting patiently for a reply to my last letter from the learned RAM CHANDRA and the 4,000 Adyapaks of the *Shradh*. I have added another challenge in my closing letter, but here I only repeat my former one, which, insignificant as it may appear, is really a challenge to all the Pundits of Bengal to show that they understand their own sacred literature, and are able to defend it at the bar of modern science. If none of them—not even "the modern RAM CHANDRA" himself—can come forward and bend this bow of a Western Janaka, let the champions of Hindu idolatry henceforth "hide their diminished heads" before the more powerful scholars of Europe, and let the last abominations of that idolatry, even in these Durga Pujah days, slink into outer darkness and shame.

I publicly repeat my challenge, and shall only say that until the close of the Durga Pujah,—when I hope my letters will have been diligently studied, "*I pause for a reply.*"

W. HASTIE.

The General Assembly's Institution.

October 13, 1882.

## XV. EUROPEAN VERSIONS OF HINDOO DOCTRINES.

### To the Editor.

Sir,—The solution of riddles and conundrums is not a legitimate subject for the columns of the *Statesman*, and if I again seek to occupy any portion of its space, it is not with a view to essay my skill in exercises which Mr. Hastie may possibly have found beyond the capacity of unpromising students in the General Assembly's Institution. The courage and dash with which Mr. Hastie throws down the gauntlet I admire and acknowledge with a low *salaam*, merely suggesting, in all humility, the necessity of further improvement in transliterating and transcribing Sanskrit texts. Contempt for diacritical marks is no doubt right, but I am afraid that, without them, even Dr. Muir himself will not acknowledge the mutilated fragment to be Vedic verse.

But Mr. Hastie's letter of the 6th has a serious as well as a comic side. Mr. Hastie now ascends from the apostolic serenity of his former letters, to the grandeur of prophetic fury. It is no longer St. Paul addressing the benighted heathen in the language of persuasion ; it is the old Hebrew prophet hurling forth anathemas against the enemies of God and of Israel. In plain language, as some irreverent heathen may be supposed to say, *Mr. Hastie loses temper.* That is an important point gained in favor of Hinduism. Mr. Hastie attacks, without any provocation, the proceedings, in a solemn mourning ceremony held in the private dwelling-house of one of the most respectable Hindu families in the country ; attacks all the most respected members of native society ; attacks their religion ; attacks the religion of the nation. And all this without the slightest provocation, and from no other motive than a somewhat overflowing zeal in the cause of truth and of religion.

And then, when an humble individual of the nation whose religion he tramples upon, ventures upon a single retort, Mr. Hastie's temper is on fire, and it explodes. The combatant who loses his temper in fight is rarely believed to be on the winning side. That is the point I score in favor of Hinduism. If this is the attitude which the Christian missionary of the present day thinks it proper to assume towards Hinduism, Hinduism has nothing to fear from his labours.

But to come to the real *casus belli*, which alone is of any importance. I suggested to Mr. Hastie that before putting himself forward as the assailant of the Hindu religion, he should study the Hindu scriptures in the original, and under the guidance of native scholars who believe in them. That Mr. Hastie does not choose to accept my advice does no harm either to me or to my cause. It is no loss to the Hindu religion that its assailants do not choose to be better armed than they are. But beneath Mr. Hastie's scornful rejection of my advice, there lurk errors which are not confined to him, but are shared by a large class of Europeans, whose numbers, position and influence, and sincere good feeling for Indian populations give them an importance far superior to what can arise out of this shallow and somewhat worn-out controversy.

The first of these errors consists in the assumption that, because European Sanskritists are competent scholars, the translations from Sanskrit which they produce must necessarily teach all that the originals have to teach. A brief consideration will convince Mr. Hastie, and others who think with him, that no translation from the Sanskrit into a European language can truly or even approximately represent the original.

Let the translator be the profoundest Sanskrit scholar in the world—let the translation be the most accurate that language can make it, still the disparity between the original and the translation will be, for practical purposes, very wide. The reason is obvious. You can translate a word by a word, but behind the word there is an idea, the thing which the word denotes, and this idea you cannot translate, if it does not exist among the people in whose language you are translating. The English or the German language can possess no words or expressions to denote ideas or conceptions which have never entered into a Teutonic brain. Now, a people so thoroughly unconnected with England or Germany as the old Sanskrit speaking people of India, and developing a civilisation and a literature peculiarly their own, had necessarily a vast store of ideas and conceptions utterly foreign to the Englishman or the German, just as the Englishman or the German boasts a still vaster number of ideas utterly foreign to the Hindu. These which form the spirit and the matter of religious and philosophical treatises, are entirely distorted and, as a matter of necessity, misrepresented in every translation—even in the best. And the best translations —not translations merely, but all comments and expositions in any language so widely differing as the the European languages differ from the Sanskrit—must, thus, to a great extent be misleading.

And who is best qualified to expound the ideas and conceptions which cannot be translated—the foreigner who has nothing corresponding to them in the whole range of his thoughts and experiences, or the native who was nurtured in them from his infancy ? If obviously the latter, what is the meaning of this towering indignation at my suggestion that Mr. Hastie should resort to the latter for instruction ? I added that he should take his lessons not merely from a Brahmin, but from a Brahmin who *believed* in them. Was it so very unreasonable as to call down a protest from Mr. Hastie on behalf of the helpless, illtreated scholars of Europe ? Does Mr. Hastie believe that any department of human thought which has had its influence on a large portion of the human race, will yield any valuable results without a loving and reverential study? If Mr. Hastie thinks that he can comprehend the vast complicated labyrinth of Hindu religious belief without studying it in the original sources of knowledge, and in a spirit of patient, earnest, and reverential search after truth, he will meet with bitter disappointment. He will fail in arriving at a correct comprehension of Hinduism, as—I say it most emphatically—*as every other European who has made the attempt has failed.* And, if he thinks that his eloquence alone will enable him to demolish the oldest and the most enduring of all religions systems without a correct knowledge of its doctrines—why, I can only wish for an Indian Cervantes to record his achievements.

Mr. Hastie has unnecessarily complicated the question by his protest on behalf of European Sanskritists. No one questions their *scholarship.* I can assure him that men like Max Müller and Goldstücker, Colebrooke and Muir, Weber and Roth do not stand in need of a champion like Mr. Hastie. I yield to none in my profound respect for their learning, their ability, and the large-hearted philanthropy which leads them to devote themselves to pursuits from which my countrymen often recoil in fear and despair. And I, as a native of India, would be certainly shamefully wanting in gratitude, if I did not acknowledge their great services in the dissemination of the Sanskrit language and Sanskrit learning throughout the civilised world. When, however, Mr. Hastie goes on to say that "both the Sanskrit language and the Sanskrit literature are much better understood in Europe and America than they are in India," I decline to follow. It is, I believe, one of the most monstrous assertions ever made; but what gives it importance is that not a few Europeans, and possibly some Anglicised natives—Hindus I cannot call them—who do not mix with their own race, believe it to be true. The principal ground for this belief is, I think, to be found in the circumstance that these Europeans and natives are more familiar with what European scholars have written on Indian languages and Indian literature than with the writings of native scholars. A few natives, like Dr. Rajendralala Mitra and Dr. K. M. Banerjee, write in English. Those not less estimable men, who are more anxious to address the vast mass of their own countrymen than a few European scholars, prefer writing in their own vernacular. The existence and the scholarship of those who choose to write in their own vernacular, in preference to Mr. Hastie's, remain to him and to those who think with him as things unknown. I am also willing to confess that the native scholars have written much less than Europeans, and that the intellectual culture of the mass of the readers whom they seek to instruct being inferior to that of the highly educated class whom European writers address, the scientific value of their writings is necessarily proportionately inferior. But the inference does not follow that native scholars are less at home in the language and literature of their own country than European Sanskritists.

The question is, however, hardly relevant. European scholars may be all that Mr. Hastie says that they are ; no one seeks to depreciate their merits. What I said of them was—" They cannot teach what they do not understand ; the blind cannot lead the blind." This of course is a mere truism on the surface, but it is not the mere truism which has induced Mr. Hastie to explode. I did mean to say that the fundamental doctrines of the Hindu religion and its vast details are what no European scholar understands and what no European scholar is competent to teach. This I did mean to say, and this I again positively assert. I will add, that there are many other things in Indian literature and Indian philosophy—other things than the religious doctrines—which no European scholar understands, and no European scholar is competent to teach. I will also assert with equal emphasis that in these cases, the native scholar is decidedly a better teacher than the European. What I assert I am prepared to maintain, and if you, Mr. Editor, will not grudge me space, and your readers their patience, I will maintain what I assert in my next letter. This one is already too long.

In conclusion, I regret that having to write from a part of India accessible with difficulty, I am necessarily tardy in replying. I shall cheerfully respond to Mr. Hastie's invitation to write under "my own honest patronymic" in my concluding letter if Mr. Hastie will insist on it. That I do not do so now proceeds merely from a desire to spare Mr. Hastie the disappointment of finding himself opposed by an unworthy antagonist. In the meantime, I enclose my card, in order that Mr. Hastie may satisfy himself, at his pleasure, about the very humble position, but also about the genuine Brahminhood of his adversary.

RAM CHANDRA.

*P.S.*—The most amusing part of Mr. Hastie's letter is perhaps the parenthetical interrogation, "Did he write *Suka* ?" Mr. Hastie, who gladly recognises it "among the pearls of Sanskrit literature," does not see his way to correcting your printer's mistake. Sandilya's celebrated treatise is entitled Bhakti *Sutra*, not Bhakti *Suka*.

NOTE.—We certainly desired that this correspondence should cease ; but its intrinsic qualities, as well as Mr. Hastie's challenge require us to publish RAM CHANDRA'S letter. We shall also publish the second letter which he promises us, and then Mr. Hastie's reply, if he wishes to make one. We shall not, however, allow the single combat to grow into a *melee*.—ED., *S.*

[*Statesman*, October, 16, 1882].

## XVI. RAM CHANDRA REDIVIVUS.

### To the Editor.

Sir,—It was not without a certain "stern joy" that I discovered the valiant Ram Chandra marching out this morning, with a long column, to the defence of his own ancient windmills; although I must confess that I am deeply disappointed to find that he is not the learned Shevaite priest and protagonist of local Hinduism, that I took him to be, when I singled him out as the strongest of all my assailants for a reply. If the heroic Ram *has* an idea, it is quite evident that he can adequately express it; and I would join my request to his that you will not "grudge" him the space required for his final lucubrations, as you did with me; since there is nothing I am more desirous to see than the most competent explanation and defence of Hinduism possible, and more especially as you are good enough to promise me an opportunity afterwards for review. Till then, I shall exercise all possible self-denial in reserving anything I have to say upon the main issue; and I promise my respondent, who is so ambitious to shine as an "Indian Cervantes," that if he give us, in his best sarcastic vein, even the slightest hint of a new idea about the Sanskrit chivalry, I shall forward his productions to the great Sanskritists of Europe, whose grateful recognition—notwithstanding all he has said of them—will be prompt and generous, and of incomparably greater value to him than any humble tribute of mine. I only trust that he will not squint so wide of the riddle or conundrum as, with an astonishing irreverence for so orthodox a scion of "genuine Brahminhood," he designates the divine Vedic verse; and that he will not take the cuttle-fish for his model when he makes his final *salaam*.

In the meantime, I only beg you to allow me to correct him on *one* point, which, as being accidental to the discussion, will be more properly noticed now; and all the more that, with the characteristic logic of the special pleader, he claims to have made an initial point out of it in favour of Hinduism. The state of my temper is entirely irrelevant to the logical relations of the question, but even if it were, he can certainly claim nothing on that "score." Notwithstanding the most wanton provocation, the issues are too serious and too essentially bound up with the solemnest duty of my vocation, for me to allow any personal or private feeling to mingle with the discussion. But when the mighty Ram Chandra, like a *Deus ex machina*, in all the imposing pomp of a new *Avatar*, appeared on the scene, claiming all the wisdom of India for himself, and treating me with such contempt as would have been intolerable to "a black beetle," I deemed it quite in order to reply to him in somewhat of his own style. In my present calm mood of introspective consciousness,—and I only hope that *his* pulse is "beating as healthful music" as mine—I can honestly say that I have seldom been in better humour with *any* man, than I am at this moment with the redoubtable Ram Chandra. In my own confidential circle, be it said, his lucubrations are giving immense amusement, and, riddle or conundrum, or whatever it be, the more he writes on the subject of my challenge, the more he will amuse us. It is to myself very touching to be thus spoken to from amid the far-off echoes of the Himalayas, by this living *Vanaprastha*, or it may be even a hoary *Bhikshu* ; and I only hope that when my last letters reach him in his solitary retreat, he will not begin to think with the worthy Sir Andrew Aguecheek, "Plague on't ; an I had thought——" But perhaps the learned Ram Chandra keeps a plain Shakespeare, *if not a diacritical Veda.*

W. HASTIE.

The General Assembly's Institution,
October 16, 1882.

## XVII. THE INTELLECTUAL SUPERIORITY OF EUROPE.

### To the Editor.

Sir,—I am sorry to have again kept Mr. Hastie and his "confidential circle" waiting for the promised amusement, but a Brahman's proper occupation during the Pujas is feasting, not controversy. Advised by Mr. Hastie that religious discussions contribute so abundantly to clerical mirth, I now hasten to treat him to a rather large measure of that commodity.

What I offered to maintain in my last letter was that the fundamental doctrines of the Hindu religion, and its vast details, are what no European scholar understands, and what no European scholar is competent to teach; that this is true not only of the doctrines of the Hindu religion, but also of much in Hindu literature and Hindu philosophy, and that in these cases the native scholar is a better teacher than the European.

Your readers may consider it somewhat superfluous that anybody should undertake to prove that those who profess a religion understand its doctrines better than those who do not profess it. I must do Mr. Hastie the justice to say that he has nowhere distinctly denied this. It is, however, really the absurd conclusion to be drawn from the position Mr. Hastie has taken up. It is the logical outcome of that monstrous claim to omniscience, which certain Europeans—an extremely limited number happily—put forward for themselves. No knowledge is to them true knowledge unless it has passed through the sieve of European criticism. All coin is false coin unless it bears the stamp of a Western mint. Existence is possible to nothing which is hid from their searching vision. Truth is not truth, but noisome error and rank falsehood, if it presumes to exist outside the pale of European cognisance. The rest of mankind are the dwellers in the thick wood, says Mr. Hastie, who see not before them, and to lend sight to whom, hosts of beneficent angels have to descend from Western skies, bearing mysterious fragments of Vedic verse on their radiant wings.

Yet nothing is a more common subject of merriment among the natives of India than the Europeans' ignorance of all that relates to India. A thousand stories in illustration are current in the bazaars, one of which will admirably serve my purpose here, and I hope your readers will tolerate it. A navvy who had strayed into the country, and felt fatigued and hungry, asked for some food from a native whom he met on the way. The native gave him a cocoanut. The hungry sailor, who had never seen a cocoanut before, bit the husk, chewed it, in spite of instructions to the contrary, and finding it perfectly inedible, flung the fruit at the head of the unhappy donor in the shape of thanks. The sailor carried away with him an opinion of Indian fruits parallel to that of Mr. Hastie and others, who merely bite at the husk of Sanskrit learning, but do not know their way to the kernel within.*

---

* A REJOINDER.

TO THE EDITOR.

SIR,—Your correspondent RAM CHANDRA gives, in your issue of 21st October, an anecdote illustrative of the Europeans' ignorance of all that relates to India. Allow me to remark that it illustrates a good deal more forcibly the ignorance of the natives of India of all things European.

In the first place, a "navvy" was, I suppose, never seen in India, and certainly could not have "strayed" here. In the second place, conversation could not possibly have taken place between two men ignorant of each other's language. In the next place, a navvy is not a sailor, and would scarcely know a ship's bow from her stern. Furthermore, a sailor, as the navvy is declared to be, is of all people in the world least likely to be unacquainted wiih foreign fruits, since he sees them at every port the vessel touches at. Besides this, cocoa-nuts are to be seen and purchased at every shipping port in England, to say nothing of inland

Did the limits of this letter permit, I could advance a dozen reasons why, in the case of every country and every people, the natives must, as a necessary consequence of their being natives, understand their own language and their own literature better than any foreign student. Mr. Hastie would probably have no hesitation in admitting this, if the question were one between one European people and another. His refusal to do so, when the question is between Europeans and Hindus, is grounded upon the reason he has distinctly asserted, the intellectual superiority of Europe, the divine right of Mr. Hastie and his co-religionists to intellectual prerogatives which may not be questioned. I cheerfully admit the intellectual superiority of Europe. I deny, however, that the conclusion follows from the premises. I deny that intellectual superiority can enable any one to dispense with the essential conditions under which alone knowledge can be acquired, that it can enable the blind to see or the deaf to hear. Intellectual superiority may make a desperate bite at the husk, it cannot arrive at the kernel without the necessary native guidance.

In the case of religious doctrines, again, there is an additional reason why the native alone can be a competent teacher ; it is, that he is a believer in them. Religious doctrines are, in the absence of that faith in them which gives them their highest value, mere dead formulæ, the lifeless carcase which may yet yield

---

towns. So common are they, that they are constantly sold on stalls, in London streets, in slices, and have been ever since I was a child.

Moral No. 1.—Let not the unwary be decoyed from subjects they understand into subjects they do *not* understand. Moral No. 2.—Bazaar stories should not be accepted as even probably true, and should be enquired into before they are repeated. Can it be that RAM CHANDRA has taken his religion on trust, as he has his bazaar story ?

A LONDONER.

*Statesman*, November 6, 1882.

a lesson to the anatomist, but which is useless to the student of human nature.

Let us lay aside all general reasoning, and come to a circumstance peculiar to India, which alone is of sufficient weight to decide the case in my favour. I refer to the existence, unheeded by, or unknown to, the European, of a vast mass of *traditionary and unwritten knowledge in India*, used to supplement, illustrate, or explain the written literature. It is generally understood now that even before the art of writing was known in India, there was already a bulky literature which had to be handed down from teacher to pupil by word of mouth. Long before the introduction of writing, therefore, oral instruction had been systematised into an art such that writing could never entirely drive it out of the field. It could not do so because writing, though an undoubted convenience, was not by any means an easy art in the early stages of its existence; it was indeed never so in India even when it attained to its final perfection in the Deva Nagri character. Copying manuscripts was a work of time, and it may easily be conceived that only the substance of the doctrines to be taught was reduced to writing, the explanatory and illustrative portions being reserved for the easier method of oral communication. After this once grew into a system, it continued ever afterwards to be retained as the most convenient form of instruction, for the circumstances out of which it arose never changed. Knowledge in India thus came to be in part recorded in a written literature, and in part handed down as unwritten and traditional. All who have studied under the older generation of Bhuttacharyas of the *tols*, know, as I have the good fortune to know, that of the wealth of learning which flowed from their lips, much had no record except in the memory of the professors. This was specially the case with artistic and scientific knowledge, where another motive—professional jealousy—came into play. Each discoverer, anxious to confine to himself and his own circle the discovery at which he had arrived, never trusted it to writing, and satisfied himself with communicating it to his pupils in confidence. To this jealousy we owe that India has now utterly lost so many of her ancient arts, and so much of her ancient sciences. Medical science is a conspicuous instance; and the native physician, trained in European schools, still fails to wrest from the jealousy of the *kabiraj* treasures of knowledge which both regard as invaluable. Now all this unwritten and traditional knowledge, which is flesh and blood to the dry bones of the written literature, is wholly unavailable to the European scholar. The dry bones rattle in his hand, and as he knows how to rattle them well, they make a thundering noise in the ears of the civilised world. But the breathing form of the old learning and the old civilisation is visible to native eyes only.

I have no hesitation in admitting the decided superiority of the European enquirer in the fields of Vedic literature. To the Indian student the Vedas are dead; he pays to them the same veneration which he pays to his dead ancestors; but he does not think that he has with them any further concern. They do not represent the living religion of India, and the only interest that can be felt in them by any human being is merely the historical interest. That is all in all to the accomplished European scholar, but of little moment to the native student, who has never displayed any gifts for history. This accounts not only for the superior Vedic learning of the European, but also for the far superior value of his contributions to Indian and Aryan history. In all other departments of learning there can be no comparison between the profound but unostentatious learning of the Pundit of the *tols* with the shallow but showy acquisitions of the European professors. The rich and varied field of Indian philosophy the latter has trod but with a slight step. Into the subtle and profound Nyaya philosophy of the Bengal school, into that which formed the field on which Raghunatha, Gadadhara, Jagadisa won their great and lasting triumphs of intellect, the pride and glory of the Bengali race, he has not yet obtained a glimpse, or has obtained only the faintest glimpse. Of the great Vaishnava philosophy first formulated in that book of books—the Bhagavata Purana, and developed by a succession of brilliant thinkers, from Ramanuja to Jiva Goswami he has no adequate conception. Nothing has so largely influenced the fate of some of the Indian peoples as the Tantras, and of Tantra literature the European knows next to nothing. The secular poetry of ancient India he has studied, translated, and commented upon, but has failed to comprehend. A single hour of study of the Sakuntala by a Bengali writer, Baboo Chandranath Bose, is worth all that Europe has had to say on Kalidasa, not excepting even Goethe's well known eulogy. Hindu law, the *Smriti*, is still the almost exclusive study of the Hindus themselves. The legends of the Hindu faith, which are to the European inexpressibly silly, he has hitherto honoured only with his laughter; to the loving study of the author of *Pushpanjali* (also a Bengali writer, Baboo Bhudeb Mukerjee) they have yielded results not surpassed in loftiness and splendour by anything in European literature. And I might go on with this enumeration for columns together, but this ought to be enough. I have freely admitted European superiority where it is to be found. But their success in their special studies do not entitle the European Sanskritists to act as competent guides in departments of learning which they have not made their own.

I have been somewhat taken by surprise to find in Mr. Hastie's letter of the 16th instant, that he expects to find in this letter of mine such "explanation and defence" of Hinduism as I may be able to offer. He forgets that the issues between us exclude the larger question of the merits of Hinduism, and that in my very first letter I told him that no controversy was possible with him at present, because he did not possess the necessary qualifications.

Hinduism does not consider itself placed on its defence. In the language of lawyers, there is not yet a properly framed charge against it. And at the bar of Christianity, which itself has to maintain a hard struggle for existence in its own home. Hinduism also pleads want of jurisdiction. But I admit Mr. Hastie's right to demand an exposition of their views from those who do not accept his own. And an exposition of rational Hinduism from a native and believer will no doubt have other uses than Mr. Hastie's enlightenment. I would gladly leave this ardous task to more competent hands than mine. Even if I made the attempt, I could not accomplish it within the compass of a single letter, already long enough, and I don't think, Mr. Editor, either that you can afford space, or that I can find time for any more. It is, however, possible to close this letter with a few observations on Hinduism from the Hindu's point of view, for the benefit of those who may be inclined to study it for themselves before resolving upon its final extinction. They will at least help to illustrate, what I have advanced on the main issues in this controversy. As with these observations I positively close my share in it, I hope you will excuse the otherwise unjustifiable length to which this letter must necessarily attain.

Hinduism, like every other fully-developed religious system, consists of, *first*, a doctrinal basis or the creed ; *secondly*, a worship or rites ; and *lastly*, of a code of morals more or less dependent upon the doctrinal basis. This is the whole field of study ; but let it be well surveyed. The doctrinal basis will be found to consist in (1) *dogmas* formulated, explained, and illustrated in a mass of philosophical literature ; and (2) legends, which form the legitimate subject of the Puranas, though these encyclopædic productions contain many things other than the legends. The value of the legends is inferior to that of the philosophy, in the depths of which are laid, broad and solid, the foundations of modern Hinduism. The whole of Hindu religious philosophy is probably post-Vedic, and serves to mark the era of separation between the ancient and the modern religions of India. Each modern Hindu sect has now its own system of philosophy, but the more general conclusions of philosophy are common to all; and among all the dogmas, there is one in particular which has had more influence in shaping the destinies of India than any other. Kapila had the glory of first announcing it to the world, and the philosophy of Europe and Asia has not up to this day alighted upon a discovery grander or more fundamental than the profound distinction first made by him between matter and soul—between *purusha* and *prakriti*. In the hands of the eclectics, who are the real fathers of modern Hinduism, this great conception has taken its place as the backbone of their fabric. It runs through the whole world of Hindu thought, shaping the legends, prescribing the rites, and running through even the secular literature. So long as the student of Hinduism keeps this great idea before him, he will find Hinduism a living organism which has *grown*, and not a collection of dead formulæ lumped together by finest craft.

*Prakriti*, properly translated, is Nature. Modern science has shown what the Hindus always knew that the phenomena of nature are simply the manifestations of *force*. They worship, therefore, Nature as *force*. *Sakti*, literally and ordinarily means force or energy. As destructive energy, force is *Kali*, hideous and terrible, because destruction is hideous and terrible. As constructive energy, force is the bright and resplendent Durga. The universal soul is also worshipped, but in three distinct aspects, corresponding to the three qualities ascribed to it by Hindu philosophy. These are known in English translations as Goodness, Passion, and Darkness. I translate them as love, power and justice. Love creates, power preserves, justice dooms. This is the Hindu of Brahma, Vishnu, and Siva. I cannot stop to discuss the relation of these gods to their Vedic predecessors of the same names. The new religion grew out of the old, that time-honoured names were retained, but were grouped under new ideas. The citadel had been stormed and battered down by the Buddhists and the philosophers themselves; and had to be reconstructed out of the old materials, but on new and more solid foundations. Pantheism and polytheism, philosophy and mysticism, all lent a hand; and out of this bold eclecticism rose the beautiful religion which I do not believe to be of Divine origin, but which I accept as the perfection of human wisdom.

The great Duality—Nature and Soul—presides over all. Let us now see how the same great conception shapes the Legends. It will be enough to take for this purpose the legends of Krishna, because they are the most important, but I have time only for the briefest explanation. Krishna is Soul, Radha is Nature. The Sankhya philosophy—the school to which the great conception of Nature and Soul originally belongs but which in spite of its wealth of thought, is a gloomy pessimism—had laid down that supreme human bliss consisted in the dissociation of Soul from Nature. It had pronounced their connexion illegitimate; and the legend of Radha and Krishna retains the illegitimate connexion. Nevertheless, the Hindu worships this illicit union. He worships it because, with a truer insight than is given to the morose philosopher, he has perceived that in this union of the Soul with Nature lies the source of all beauty, all truth, and all love. And this magnificent legend, the basis of the Hindu religion, of *love for all that exists* is treated by its European critics as the grossest and most revolting story of crime ever invented by the brain of man. So much for the intellectual superiority of Europe.

I will next add an illustration to show how the same great conception runs through even the secular literature of ancient India. The Kumara Sambhava, the noblest philosophical poem to be found in any language, but, I regret to say, also one of the least understood both in India and Europe, celebrates the marriage of Nature with Soul, typified in Uma and Siva. In the hands of the great poet, the union is a legitimate one—a holy marriage. The poet could soar above both philosopher and Puranist. I regret I have not space to explain or to do justice to Kalidasa's magnificent conception; the yearning of the physical and human for the moral and the divine, and the accomplishment of their union after purification through the sacrifice of earthly desires and the discipline of the heart. In that sacrifice and in that discipline is to be found the poet's refutation of the philosopher. The sacrifice, the destruction of Kama, is narrated in a well known passage, which still remains the loftiest in all Indian literature, and is unrivalled by any I have come across in the poetry of any other nations.

I now pass on to the worship. Much of the Hindu ritual is mere mummery, admitted to be so by even the priests, and rejected with deserved contempt by educated Hindus. Mr. Hastie finds out, I hope, that the Hindu Idolatry, which is generally treated by the Christian missionary as covering the whole field of Hinduism, is really a small fraction of it and comes under consideration as a subordinate part of this second division of our subject. Mr. Hastie will probably be startled to hear that idolatry, though a part of Hinduism, is not an essential part even of the popular worship. Idol worship is permitted, is even belauded in the Hindu scriptures, but it is not enjoined as *compulsory*. The daily worship of the Hindu—his Sandhya,—his Ahnika, is not idolatrous. The orthodox Brahman is bound to worship Vishnu and Shiva every day, but he is not bound to worship their images. He may worship their images if he choose, but if he does not so choose, the worship of the Invisible is accepted as sufficient. The majority of Brahmans, I believe, do not in the daily rites go beyond this worship of the Invisible and the Unrepresented. A man may never have entered a temple and may yet be an orthodox Hindu.

And I must ask the student of Hinduism when he comes to study Hindu Idolatry, to forget the nonsense about dolls given to children. I decline to subscribe to what is simply childish, even though the authority produced is titled authority with a venerable look. The true explanation consists in the ever true relations of the subjective Ideal to its objective Reality. Man is by instinct a poet and an artist. The passionate yearnings of the heart for the Ideal in beauty, in power, and in purity, must find an expression in the world of the Real. Hence proceed all poetry and all art. Exactly in the same way the ideal of the Divine in man receives a form from him, and the form an image. The existence of Idols is as justifiable as that of the tragedy of Hamlet or of that of Prometheus. The *religious* worship of idols is as justifiable as the *intellectual* worship of Hamlet or Prometheus. The homage we owe to the ideal of the human realised in art is admiration. The homage we owe to the ideal of the Divine realised in idolatry is worship.

Nor must the student fall into the error of thinking that the image is ever taken to be the God. The God is always believed, by every worshipper, to exist apart from the image. The image is simply the visible and accessible medium through which I choose to send my homage to the throne of the Invisible and the Inaccessible. Images of gods have in themselves no sanctity. They are daily sold in the bazaars as toys. The very images worshipped are made by impure workmen, sold in the bazaars, and are treated on exactly the same footing as other shopkeeper's wares. They do not acquire any sanctity till the *prana pratistha, i.e.*, till I consent to worship it. The image is holy, not because the worshipper believes it to be his god—he believes in no such thing—but because he has made a compact with his own heart *for the sake of culture and discipline* to treat it as God's image. Like other contracts, this one with the worshipper's own heart he may terminate at his pleasure. When he terminates it, he ceases to worship the image and throws it away, as we have just thrown away by thousands the images of Durga. He could not do this if for a moment he believed it to be his God.

Our idols are hideous, say they. True, we wait for our sculptors. It is a question of art only. The Hindu pantheon has never been adequately represented in stone or clay, because India has produced no sculptors. The few good images we had have been mutilated or destroyed by the hand of Mussalman vandals. The images we worship in Bengal are, as works of art, a disgrace to the nation. Wealthy Hindus should get their Krishnas and Radhas made in Europe.

We come last of all to the ethics of the Hindu Religion. Like all other complete codes of morality, the Hindu ethical system seeks to regulate the conduct of individuals as well as the conduct of society. It is a system of ethics as well as a polity. The code of personal morality is as beautiful, if not more so, as any other in the world, not excepting the Christian; a degree of excellence which the Christian accounts for by supposing, like Mr. Hastie, that it must have been derived from Christian sources, very much after the logic of a little fellow I know, who insists that every man who drives in a carriage is his grandsire, on the ground that his grandsire drives in a carriage. The social polity is even more wonderful. It is the only system which has ever succeeded in substituting the government of Moral power in the place of that of Physical power. It is the only system which has abolished war and the military power.

If the profoundest European thinker of the nineteenth century had any acquaintance with India, he might have known that his dream of a Positive Polity and an intellectual hierarchy had, thousands of years ago, been thought out and realised with a success transcending all his anticipations.

Here, too, however, the student must distinguish between the essentials of Hinduism and its non-essential adjuncts. Much of the ethical portion is pure ethics, and not religion. The social polity is also non-essential. Caste, therefore, which is the most prominent feature of that polity, is non-essential. There have been and there still are many Hindu sects who discard caste distinctions. The Chaitanyaite Vaishnavas furnish an instance in point.

Mr. Hastie may turn round upon me here and say "You strip Hinduism of its rites, its idolatry, its caste ; what do you then leave it ?" I leave *the kernel without the husk.*

I have done. I hope Mr. Hastie now understands how I dispose of his challenge. The modern Ram Chandra turns away from the Western Janaka's bow without touching it even with the tip of his little finger. For, alas! the new Janaka has no Janaki to offer as the prize. Truth, the Janaki he seeks to win, must be wooed in another fashion. Methods of disputation which find favor only among pugnacious schoolboys gathered at a wedding feast are as unworthy of Mr. Hastie as they are of me. But if a confession from me of inferiority to Western scholars in Vedic learning will bring any comfort to Mr. Hastie, he will see that I have already made such confession on behalf of my countrymen, and I even more readily make it on my own behalf. I make no pretension to scholarship of any kind.

I have to thank Mr. Hastie for his very kind offer to procure for my lucubrations the recognition of the great Sanskritists of Europe. I assure Mr. Hastie that he has again mistaken his man. Happy that such recognition is already the fortunate lot of certain *distinguished* countrymen of mine, whom I somewhat reluctantly spare the humiliation of being mentioned by name in this connection. I hasten to assure Mr. Hastie that I am not ambitious of honours which I do not deserve and may not prize. As my card is already at Mr. Hastie's disposal, I may presume to tell him that the approbation of a whole people has consoled me during a quarter of a century, and may console me still, for the absence of laurels which more fitly grace the heads that wear them now. If Mr. Hastie knows anything of Hinduism, he knows that the Hindu places the wreath round the full, not round the empty, vessel. I am sorry to have to say this, but Mr. Hastie's pointless jest carries an insinuation which can be met only in this way.

In conclusion I have to thank you for allowing me the very unreasonable extent of space which I have taken up; I have also to express my deep commiseration for Mr. Hastie's bitter disappointment in finding that Ram Chandra was not the very great man from whose encounter he had expected to add fresh lustre to his rusty arms. There is however nothing like hope. Let him cheer up. A louder and shriller blast at the castle-gate of Hinduism may yet procure him the honour of an encounter with even—ay, even with the windmills.

RAM CHANDRA.

---

## XVIII. THE INTELLECTUAL INFERIORITY OF INDIA.

### To the Editor.

SIR,—I had almost forgotten the modern mirth-provoking RAM CHANDRA, in a more serious study of his immortal ideal—the heroic Ram of " happy memory" ; and was beginning to think he had sunk into as deep an oblivion of himself, of his surroundings, and of his engagements, as the famous seven Sleepers of Ephesus, or the more kindred Rip Van Winkle. Here he is, however, all alive again this morning, with his ancient worn-out habits still upon him, and causing no little wonder, I doubt not, to your sensible readers by his two columns of strange rhetoric and antiquated jargon. He tells us as his excuse for delay that, although he has himself discarded the popular religion as a mere *husk* unworthy of the literary idol of the millions, who has been feeding for a quarter of a century like a Hindu god, on the sweet essence of *kernels*, he has been busy,—genuine Brahman as he is, and in accordance with the accommodating code of morals he defends,—" feasting" at the feet of the " inaccessible" goddess of the time. It is but too sadly evident however, that *his* faithfulness to the dying faith has had no reward, and that *Ma Durga*, if she *did* come, as her votaries believe, in all her might and splendour from the heavenly heights to look upon her offerings, passed all his coldly by. Not upon his sacrificial knife at least fell the twinkle of the eye of the awful Durga. His pen is even more *wooden* than before ; and if the goddess, who is believed to embody his eternal Prakriti, had brought a favor for *him*, it would have certainly been a low whisper in his ear, that for *her* sake, as well as for his own, only his " *silence*" *could* become " golden."

I have certainly no wish to be unjust to the chivalric RAM CHANDRA, for whose utterance I began waiting with a great expectation; but I must admit that he is right in thinking that, in one sense at least, I am completely disappointed with this defence of his religion. If modern Hinduism can, indeed, say no more than this for itself, it must be evident to all that it is only with the foolish prejudices and worse corruptions of a childish and sensual people, that we Missionaries are contending, and not with the spiritual force of a living and intellectual faith. If this shallow verbosity, this inconsistent farrago of phrases, this total irrelevance of reasoning, this feeble commonplace of reflection, this utter ignorance of even the rudiments of Hindu mythology and philosophy, is to be taken as the highest exposition of the religion of the educated Hindu, then tell it not in Europe, publish it not in America, but let more earnest men try to give it "the happy dispatch" as soon as possible, or let it at once end by a *felo de se*, that it may show its face in public no longer. It will surprise me if the more learned representatives of Hinduism—for there *are* such—do not publicly repudiate RAM CHANDRA as an unbidden intruder into this controversy, and as no chosen champion of theirs. They will say that, if he is anything, he is a romancer and not a reasoner; an Anglicist and not a Sanskritist; an apostate and not an apologist; a poetaster and not a critic. But they would do him wrong if they imagined they could do anything essentially better, or more really effective, in the cause. Had the abler men whom he names—Dr. Rajendra Lala Mitra or Baboo Bhudeb Mookerjee—come to the rescue, they would not have written better English; but they would have been more cautious, more correct, and less vulnerable in their utterances and theories. Certainly the apology of RAM CHANDRA is not worth sending to any of the Sanskrit scholars of Europe for its own sake, unless it were to show them what an air of mystery can be thrown over the most elementary conceptions of Hinduism, which have been among their commonplaces for a century, and how very little even the best educated Hindus have yet profited by their devotion and their discoveries. It is certainly not too much to say—and I am sure every orthodox Hindu will agree with me—that the vague allegations about *ignorance* of Hinduism may now be most justly brought home only to himself; that in so far as he *does* understand it, he entirely abandons it; that his public *defence* of it has only exposed its utter weakness and untenableness; and that his own relation to Hinduism is that of the wildest *heterodoxy,* grounded—it is most incredible to learn —upon the most thorough-going *Atheism* that Hindu philosophy has known. These are strong statements, but the competent reader of RAM CHANDRA'S letters will already have recognised that they can *all* be proved against him to a domonstration.

There is a too evident mass of logical contradictions and literary blunders scattered over the surface of RAM CHANDRA'S letters, which, however, in order to spare your space, I shall at present pass over entirely. You closed your columns against me with matters of far more importance than the trivialities of RAM CHANDRA, and however much it might amuse your readers, I have no desire to merely humiliate that distinguished writer, and I am most desirous to economise my words for my own sake. But when I edit RAM CHANDRA'S letters in the small volume which, in spite of myself, is growing under my hands out of this controversy, I shall take care to indicate these points in brief foot-notes, so that he may in good time claim back his own again with usury. He will be put right about the relation of Shiva to the Vedas, and of the "navvy" to the sailor; about the Bhagavat Purana and the Kumara Sambhava and Dr. Muir, &c.; and will even find a considerable amount of valuable information about Hinduism from the greatest authorities, which he will do well to study with great care before he undertakes to write upon the subject again. In the meantime, knowing that I am limited by you in my reply, I shall gather together all the cardinal points in RAM CHANDRA'S contention, not complaining even of his shifting the question from my ground of controversy, but taking him as I find him, and discussing him as briefly as I can. If I do not waste much time upon so incompetent and ill-equipped a controversialist, it is mainly because I most honestly think it is not worthwhile; but I shall be ready to deal at greater length, if required, with any more plausible defence of Hinduism, if such be forthcoming. The following are, so far as I can gather them, all the positions put forward by RAM CHANDRA, and with which I have now to deal :—

1. His fundamental axiom that none can possibly understand a religious system or doctrine but those in whose language its literature is written.—2. His cardinal view that no one can understand or expound a religious or philosophical fact, unless he believes in it to begin with.—3. His heterodox theory that the Vedas are *not* the authoritative scriptures of the Hindu religion, but are now a dead letter of no importance to the Hindus, and are at best but a literary curiosity "to the accomplished European scholar," to whom he at the same time makes a most astonishing concession.—4. His remarkable discovery of a "vast mass of *traditionary and unwritten knowledge in India* which is wholly unavailable to the European scholar," but which is "used to supplement, illustrate, or explain the written literature."—5. His still more remarkable discovery that the fundamental doctrine of the Hindu religion lies in the atheistical principle of the Sankhya philosophy.—6. His repeated assertion that no European Sanskritist has ever understood, or is even able to understand, the ultimate principle of Hinduism as discovered by Kapila, and illustrated by his followers.—7. His practical allegation, that

RAM CHANDRA Redivivus has for the first time expounded the great mystery of the Hindu religion, and has expounded it in *English* although that splendid feat could not possibly have been accomplished by any English scholar, owing to his inability to wield his own too limited and imperfect vernacular for the purpose ;—and, further, that this same distinguished Bengali and thoroughly "Anglicised native," who must henceforth be prominently immortalised in all histories of Sanskrit literature and Indian thought, has at the same time thoroughly understood the numerous European expositions of the Sankhya system in English, French, German, Italian and Latin, notwithstanding his own fundamental canon of criticism, and *knows them to be all wrong.*—9. His gratifying assurance that idolatry, though a very "subordinate part of Hinduism, is not an essential part *even of the popular worship.*"—10. His bold assertion that from his own knowledge of the state of mind of "every (Hindu) worshipper," "the image is never taken to be the god," and that its being sold in the bazaars and thrown away at the close of the Pujah, is a proof that the idolater does not believe it to be a god.—11. His still bolder declaration that he himself does not believe the Hindu religion "to be of Divine origin," but that he accepts it only "as the perfection of human wisdom."—12. His highly philosophical conception that, having stripped Hinduism "of its rites, its idolatry, its caste, he leaves *the kernel without the husk*" ; and that Auguste Comte is to be regarded as "the profoundest European thinker of the Nineteenth Century."—13. And finally, to make up the famous dozen, his extraordinary hallucination in thinking, as he takes off his armour, that he has expounded, or defended *Hinduism*, and that any form of Hinduism *could* survive such exposition and defence. These 13 articles really constitute the creed of RAM CHANDRA, and if they do not include every thing he has said, they at least contain everything he has said that could possibly be regarded as of importance. The mere statement in plain terms of this strange jumble of ancient heterodoxy, mediæval sensualism, and modern scepticism, must be its own refutation to all competent and earnest thinkers; but as this is just the creed—if it can be so called—of the largest section of the educated Hindus at present, a few remarks may be allowed on each point, not merely with the view of shooting RAM CHANDRA'S "folly as it flies," but in the hope of also reaching the flighty fancies of too many like him, even now everywhere upon the wing.

1. The first point need not detain us long. There is undoubtedly an antecedent probability that any literature will be best understood by the people whose most gifted sons have produced it, and in whose language it is written; but the exceptions to the contrary in the history of literature are so numerous that it cannot be raised into anything like a universal rule. And when we look at the cases in detail, there is none to which it is so inapplicable as that very Sanskrit literature in its most important elements, as RAM CHANDRA himself is forced by the logic of fact to admit. The position upon which he grounded his axiom in his second letter, was that *no translation* can represent the ideas contained in another language, and on this account "no European scholar is competent to teach" what is contained in Sanskrit. But he evidently forgets that these European scholars do not study Sanskrit through the medium of translations, but at the fountain heads of all its streams, and that many of them, like those he has named, are as familiar with all its fulness of vocables and all its complexities of construction as they are with their own tongue, and in this respect they have an enormous advantage over the native pundits, from their far wider range of reading and their more scientific method of study. If this theory of RAM CHANDRA

were correct, the real contents of the Sanskrit literature would be proved to be long since unintelligible and unavailable to the world at large, and not merely to the European. Sanskrit is a dead language, and every student, be he native or not, can only get at its contents in the same way, or not at all. The Bengali has only a slight relative advantage over the European in the nearer relation, of his vernacular to the Sanskrit; but on RAM'S principles it must be as impossible to translate Sanskrit ideas into Bengali, as into Greek, or Latin, or German, or English; and it is really found to be in fact often much more difficult. He must himself then, along with all the pundits, share in the ignorance and incompetency which he so rashly attributes to the European Sanskritists, unless he had been delivered from them by a Divine revelation in Sanskrit itself, which he would be the very last man apparently to claim. And when we test his axiom by the appeal to history, it breaks down in every case, and most conspicuously in the case of Sanskrit. Even the English have had to admit that their own unapproached Shakespeare has been better understood in the Nineteenth Century by the Germans than by themselves. But in return, it may be claimed that Carlyle penetrated more deeply into Goethe, and that Lewes wrote a more appreciative life of the great poet of the century than did any of his own countrymen. And so it has been with the Goethe of Italy, and the Shakespeare of Spain, and many other kindred instances. And to press the fact nearer Sanskrit, it may most confidently be asserted that the classical literature of ancient Greece and Rome are even now better understood in their inmost spirit and meaning than they ever were by any Greek or Roman reader of the old world. And the same holds even truer of the Sanskrit language and literature as I formerly asserted in the interests of truth, although it appeared at first sight to RAM CHANDRA, "one of the most monstrous assertions ever made." During the ten days of study required for the production of his second letter, he seems, however, to have gradually come to see the unpalatable fact in its true light, and he now writes with more moderation and wisdom, that he has "no hesitation in admitting the decided superiority of the European enquirer in the field of Vedic literature." But it is certainly an axiom that "the greater includes the less," and if the superiority of the European enquirer be so candidly admitted in the far more difficult department which also dominates all the easier and the less, how shall his inferiority be consistently maintained where superiority is already pratically won? The truth is that RAM CHANDRA does not understand the first principles of literary criticism, and has not obtained the slightest glimpse of the great law that obtains between productive and reproductive thought. Although it may sound as a paradox at first, it is certain that no literature, nor any spontaneous outburst of genius, is completely understood by the people among whom it arose, nor is fully appreciated until it is dead. The energy and enthusiasm of production in the great artist, work rather like a controlling instinct than a conscious reflection, and the people whose possession it becomes are too much overpowered by its spell to measure it calmly or see it fairly on all its sides. And it is only when it is taken up in the light of history that its mode of production and its power are really discovered, and that it passes from the limited apprehension and tenure of the people that produced it, into the universal possession and enjoyment of mankind at large. This cosmopolitan interpretation of the old, which is now in full movement, will evidently be the final originality of the work of thought and probably its consummation. That the ancient Sanskrit literature has been found able to pass through this process is the highest thing that can now be said of it ; but the scholars who have given it this cosmopolitan value and currency were not the purblind pundits of the later Bengal, but the widevisioned Sanskritists of Europe, who first discovered its universal historical filiation and its living significance. And their error has rather been, and is, to exaggerate the value of their discoveries, and to encourage the expectation that far more is to come out of Sanskrit than it can ever possibly yield. But it is a generous error like that of the discoverer of the new-old world, who saw in it a greater good for his country than it could bring; and it is surely nobler than the opposite blunder of the native who has never seen beyond the horizon of his birth-day, and who would measure the march of the world by the narrow lines of his own primitive and decaying civilisation. RAM CHANDRA'S axiom is not only thoroughly false as a treason to the common humanity of the rational mind, but history most completely disproves it, and even if it did not, it would not only not support his contention but reduce it to an irrational impossibility.

I fear that you will not allow me to go further to-day, but I shall endeavour to-morrow to touch on the remaining points as briefly as I can.

W. HASTIE.

---

*( Continuation. )*

TO THE EDITOR.

SIR,—2. The second cardinal doctrine in RAM CHANDRA'S creed is that no one can understand or expound a religious or philosophical fact, unless he *believe* in it, to begin with. This is what Theologians call a *formal* principle, but it is of great importance in determining the material of a system. And RAM CHANDRA, seeing this, finds in it the chief disqualification of the European Sanskritists, with all their admitted learning, for any competent apprehension or exposition of his Hinduism. Whether he is himself entitled to claim any higher qualification on this ground we shall afterwards see, and as regards the *principle* itself, a few words will suffice. It is certainly not a new one, and RAM CHANDRA can assuredly lay no claim to any originality regarding it. Apart from its reiterated assertion in the Brahmanical system, it received a very complete discussion in the European schools of Theology in the Middle Ages. They were indeed entirely divided into two sections by their relation to it—the Dogmatists holding that Faith is subsidiary to Knowledge, and taking as their motto—"*Believe* that you may *know*" (*crede ut intelligas*): the Rationalists holding that Knowledge is subsidiary to Faith, and taking as their motto: "*Know* that you may *believe*" (*intellige ut credas*). For myself, I consider that they were both wrong, but it is unnecessary to discuss the question in this connection on its philosophical grounds and merits. It is enough to observe that RAM CHANDRA holds the least tenable of the two theories; and that almost all the thought of the modern world is opposed to him, and especially that very positive school of philosophy to which he glories in giving his allegiance. It is now recognised to be the principle of all religious obscurantism, and the sheet-anchor of every surviving superstition. RAM CHANDRA, however, does not grasp the principle in its deeper bearing, and is consequently quite unaware of his own inconsistency with himself. With him it is really no more than a paltry *petitio principii* brought in surreptitiously in order, if possible, to save something for the pundits out of the spoils of Sanskrit learning. Even in this flimsy and limited aspect, it will however not bear a moment's inspection. There is no body of men so much divided in their beliefs and no-beliefs as the pundits, and yet they will all pronounce as oracularly as RAM CHANDRA himself, on any question pertaining to Hinduism. Who is to decide which of them has the right belief, and consequently the right knowledge? On this ground, whatever absurdity any one may profess to *believe* about any subject, must, when expounded by him, be received as the very deepest truth about that subject. If Ram Chandra *believes* that I have as many arms as Ravana, and writes it down in his next composition, nobody who sees me with two only, need bring the evidence of sense or reason to bear against his representation! The Hindu faith is in fact living upon this very principle of antecedent credulity; but notwithstanding Ram Chandra's advocacy it will not be able to live upon it much longer. In all the European schools of science it has now been once for all discarded as a canon of criticism and no one could give a more convincing proof of the unscientific character of his system than by claiming anything for it, on the ground of his own hereditary unreasoned belief, or demanding that others should begin by believing in it as the condition of its being made intelligible to them. The formal principle advanced by Ram Chandra, as an evasion of knowledge and an asylum for ignorance, is thus repudiated by all the science of the time, including the school of his profoundest thinker of the century, and nowhere, more logically than by the ancient Sankhya system of philosophy, under whose banners he expounds and defends modern Hinduism. And certainly nothing is to be gained by him or any other from this principle—even if it could be established, which it manifestly could not, except with those who *cannot* or *will not* think. It is to be hoped, therefore, that *this* ground will not be taken again by those who would attempt to prove an inferiority of insight on the part of European scholars, since they well know what value to put upon the subterfuge.—But while thus rejecting Ram Chandra's principle as exploded and illegitimate, the *true* relation between enquiring thought and the intelligibility of a religious system may be stated in a word. It is simply this, that while the votary of any religion generally understands his own system better than he does any other, the follower of any other religion which has outgrown it, or which moves on a higher stage of thought, understands it much better than he does, and is much more competent to expound its meaning and relations. This is only an application of a general law of mind, that the more highly it is developed, and the more widely it is cultured, the clearer and the deeper is its insight into things. The man understands the child better than the child understands himself. Knowledge of the mode of development in the higher organisms explains the lower. The progressive present furnishes the only key for opening up the mysteries of the past. Thus the Hindu is able to understand the religions of the aboriginal tribes better than they do themselves, and to explain his own convincingly to them ; and in like manner the educated Brahmo, and still more, the educated Christian, understands Hinduism better than the Hindu himself, although he may not be fully acquainted with all its detail of beliefs and rites, because he knows exactly wherein it falls short of his own higher faith, and every sensuous relapse from that more spiritual standpoint brings him sensibly nearer in experience to its practical side. If RAM CHANDRA will ponder this principle carefully, he will see the ground upon which I logically claim for the European scholars in their new science of Comparative Theology, not only that superiority of learning regarding the scriptures of Hinduism which he admits, but a far deeper understanding of their ultimate meaning, and a far greater competency to explain them to the literary world, than all the orthodox Hindus can possibly possess. And in asserting this, I do not hold the extreme view of Renan, that it is a condition of explaining any religion to have survived a faith in them all, but rather consider that an intelligent faith in the absolute religion, which is Christianity, is related to the other faiths of the world somewhat as anthropology is related to palæontology. And I would even admit that some of the Christian students of comparative theology understand Hinduism and similar ethnic religions, to whose study they give almost all their energy of thought, better than they do their own Christianity; just as the workman is often comparatively ignorant of his own measures and instruments, and as a naturalist may be a better geologist than an anthropologist, because the lower forms are much more easy to understand and expound.

3. The extraordinary heresy of RAM CHANDRA, the apologist, about the Vedas is very startling and perplexing. As everybody should know, it is a fundamental doctrine of every Hindu sect and of every Hindu system (except the coarse sensualism of the Charvakas, which seems to be reviving), that the Vedas are the supreme, inspired, authoritative source of all truth, and that the worst of all heresies consists in rejecting them. For the evidence of this doctrine readers need not go further than the third volume of Dr. Muir's *Sanskrit Texts*, where it is presented with his characteristic accuracy of scholarship and impartiality of judgment. And even the Sankhya system, although most radically opposed to them in principle, takes great pains by all sorts of ingenious evasions, to harmonise its claims with the inspiration of the Vedas. But here is what this would-be Kapila, in the form of the latest defender of the traditional faith, now proclaims. "To the Indian student *the Vedas are dead*; he pays to them the same veneration which he pays to his dead ancestors; *but he does not think that he has with them any further concern. They do not represent the living religion of India, and the only interest that can be felt in them by any human being is merely the historical interest.* This is all in all to the accomplished European scholar, but of little moment to the native student who has never displayed any gifts for history." And then comes his remarkable concession to the European scholar, "This accounts not only for the superior Vedic learning of the European, but also for the *far superior value of his*

*contributions* to Indian and Aryan history."—I shall not weaken the impression of this extraordinary statement by dwelling upon it. It is analogous to what would be the procedure of a Christian apologist—if we could suppose such a thing—who should begin his defence of Christianity by declaring the Bible to be "dead" and of no living interest to the Christian as regards his religion. It shews how hopelessly modern Hinduism has lost its bearings and how illogical it has become. It is this which drives men like RAM CHANDRA to *postulate* a faith in Hinduism as the condition of understanding it, under which cover they may make it out to be *anything* they choose. The only logical criterion that *could* be applied to determine the correctness of any representation of Hinduism *must* be the Vedic "law and testimony." But RAM CHANDRA has learned how the great European scholars have shown the utter groundlessness of the extravagant claims made for the Vedas, how they have disproved their alleged Divineness and inspiration from themselves, how they have proved them to be utterly unintelligible to the modern Hindu and entirely inapplicable to the social conditions of modern Hiudu life, and how the supposed "great thoughts that wandered through eternity" have dissolved under their scientific tests into the simple but lofty fancies of a primitive Aryan tribe. And with this knowledge he is perplexed, for it has withdrawn the whole foundation upon which his religion has been reared; and in his perplexity, he abandons it to the European in despair. And nothing is left for him but to try to construct the modern Hinduism out of itself, and even to begin to build it *downwards* from its own airy copestone, which is faith. To him the lascivious Tantras, which one might suppose, without any wrong to Hinduism, to have been written by a race of monkeys under the omniscient superintendence of the all-wise Hanuman, becomes the inspired Book of books, and what the wily old Brahmans out of a concession to the popular sensuality dignified as "*a fifth Veda*," swallows up all the rest in its disgusting maw, and becomes the bloated idol of the modern Hindu, as it is the blighting curse of his heart and of his home. Let him work out more fully the picture of this degrading Belial and Moloch, as "Lust hard by hate," in fancied superiority to the pure faith of the European scholars, not indeed as "of Divine origin" for no one could be bold enough now to attempt that, but even as "the perfection of human wisdom"—*if he dare.*

4. But RAM CHANDRA superadds to his principle of blind belief and his Tantric Bible, his "vast mass of *traditionary and unwritten knowledge in India* which is wholly unavailable to the European scholar," but which is "used to supplement, illustrate or explain the written literature." In this again there is nothing peculiar to India about the fact, except that it is here of incomparably less importance than in almost any other country, from the grotesque and irrational character of most of the traditions referred to, and because the passion for literary composition, which is eminently characteristic of the Hindu, has really embodied and preserved in the ocean af Sanskrit writing almost everything that is of value. If it be really otherwise, then RAM CHANDRA and the Hindu *litterateurs* he refers to, would be much more usefully employed than in mere shallow imitations of English novelists, in gathering up any such fragments of floating tradition as might be auxiliary to the work of European scholars in their new scientific treatment of Aryan "Folklore." But beyond this, it can have *no* value, and least of all as a rational supplement or defensive buttress to religious Hinduism. In his own exposition of the Hindu religion, RAM CHANDRA makes no use of his "discovery," as if he had forgotten it the very moment after he had hit upon it. Or if he drew "the flesh and blood of the breathing form" in which he has presented the Sankhya philosophy from this illustrative museum, it would have been well, as we shall see, had he

also obtained a subtle opiate from the mysterious treasures of his *kabirajes* to administer to his readers when he proceeded to exhibit it in public. No orthodox Hindu will allow *any* value to this supposed source of higher knowledge, nor would the Sankhya even admit it into its department of "legitimate testimony." This addendum would at the best reduce the evidence for Hinduism to the gross creations of the popular imagination and the dim forgetfulness of mere hearsay. But the Divineness of the true religion breathes in the pure ether of heaven's own light and cannot grovel in the nasty slubber of the filthy stye. Let RAM CHANDRA, therefore, at some other time, make out of it, for his popular Hinduism, as "the perfection of human wisdom," *what he will.*

I find again that I must break off at this point, but to-morrow I shall certainly close these communications, by a few remarks on RAM CHANDRA'S view of the Sankhya philosophy and all else that still remains to be reviewed.

W. HASTIE.

The General Assembly's Institution,
October 29, 1882.

---

*(Conclusion.)*

TO THE EDITOR.

SIR,—5. The positions advanced by RAM CHANDRA regarding the Sankhya, are as extraordinary as his view of the Vedas; and they are evidently regarded by himself as his strongest points. The first of these, so far as I have gathered it, is the very "remarkable discovery that the fundamental doctrine of the Hindu religion lies in the atheistical principle of the Sankhya philosophy." If this were true, there could be nothing more remarkable even to a Positivist, whether from the philosophical or the historical point of view. The *atheistical* character of the Sankhya system is beyond dispute. On *this* point, all the authorities worth referring to, Hindu and European, are practically agreed. I have gone over the Sutras, and read the best expositions with care, and can see no other view open to a genuine historical criticism. There is no place for God in a system which professes to evolve *all* things logically out of a primordial matter except individual souls, which are indeed eternal, but are *not* God. The attempts of the author and his followers to evade the popular antipathy to bald atheism, by an inconsistent recognition of the Vedas, and a verbal acknowledgment of certain popular divinities, are more transparent and unreal than even the similar efforts of the Epicureans. Dr. Rajendralala Mitra has dignified the Sankhya too much by calling it "the *hylotheistic* philosophy"; had he known Greek a tithe as well as he knows Sanskrit, he would have more correctly designated it "the hylo-*zoistic* philosophy." The very fact of the distinctively *theistic* charactor of the rival Yoga branch of Patanjali, reflects the conscious aversion to the atheism of Kapila. And perhaps, after all, RAM CHANDRA has dimly seen this, through the vague cloud of his modern positivism; and the striking resemblance in *negative* points of Kapila to Comte, is no doubt regarded by him as the chief excellence of the Hindu philosopher. And yet, were the relations of Kapila what he supposes, they would be more than wonderful. Comte's atheistical "Religion of Humanity" was the more sentimental dream of a diseased brain, and his healthier followers have laughed this silly adjunct of his system to scorn. But the principle which Kapila is said to have first expounded, is declared to have become the central doctrine of modern Hinduism, so that the religion of the millions of India, for a thousand years at least, has been at heart as godless as Buddhism, and took its rise, according to RAM CHANDRA, not from the religion of the Vedas, but in the nihilistic speculation of an ancient Hindu Bradlaugh. Surely, this "remarkable discovery" is more degrading to the popular polytheism than my representation of it as a "*superstitious* atheism," for it makes its atheism a conscious worship of brute "force," and most other Hindus will be ready indignantly to disclaim it. And yet it is nearer the truth than anything else RAM CHANDRA has said; and its main blunder is merely a historical one about Kapila, wrapped in a cloud of words that would prevent most readers from seeing the underlying fact in all its naked deformity. To Kapila and to RAM CHANDRA, what the speculative reason of the Hindus found at the end of its search, as the last and deepest fact of the universe, was alas! according to the grim and gloomy Richter—only "*an eyeless socket*."

6. And it is said, or rather vociferated again and again, that no European has been able to comprehend or expose this profoundest system of philosophy. But here, again, with other ten days' study, RAM CHANDRA would be too honest not to make another similar concession to the gifts and the achievement of the European scholars. That "intellectual superiority of Europe," which has surmounted all the difficult heights of the Vedas, was not likely to give way before the smooth, easy pathways of the philosophical aphorisms. It would be mere waste of time to reproduce the proof of this in detail. Dr. K. M. Banerjea is in fact the only native scholar of the modern world who has not only dealt with the ancient philosophy of his country with competent critical power, but has reached and led upon the highest altitude; and we are proud to claim the fact as an earnest of what Christianity can still accomplish in the clear, decisive, spiritual working of the Hindu mind. The pundits have really done nothing but repeat and repeat, and repeat yet again, *memoriter*, like the boys in their mechanical vociferations in a Bengali *patshala*; they have not thrown a

single ray of light upon the origin, or the principle, or the validity of even the popular Sankhya Sutras. But the European scholars—Colebrooke, Roer, Ballantyne, Hall, Müller, Weber, Cowell, Gough, Davies, and others—have mastered the whole subject, and put its every aspect into clearest light. The Sankhya philosophy is in fact now as thoroughly understood in Europe and America, as are the sensationalism of Locke and the evolutionism of Darwin, with which it has indeed very striking affinities.

7. Does only RAM CHANDRA then, of all scholars and thinkers, understand and expound the Sankhya? Surely nothing more ludicrous could be maintained even by himself, than *that*. What a contrast between his meddling, and muddling, and the learning and lucidity of the following concise summary by Dr. Banerjea: "The Nyaya and the Sankhya are in fact a sort of compromise between Brahminism and Buddhism. They contain as much of the Buddhist element, as could be held without danger to Brahminical supremacy. . . . The objects of knowledge are according to Kapila's arrangement, twenty-five. *Prakriti* or Nature defined to be the equipoise of the three qualities of *excellence*, *foulness*, and *darkness*, is the first, as *Purusha*, or Soul, is the last. The intervening twenty-three are *mahat* or intelligence, *ahankara* or self-consciousness, the five *tanmatra* or subtle elements, eleven organs, inclusive of the mind, and the five gross elements. Of these, Prakriti, *the rootless root*, *is the first cause of all things*, while Purusha or soul *is a simple witness*. Both are eternal, but the former, inanimate and and non-sentient, is prolific and active; the latter intelligent and sentient, is non-productive because free and indifferent. Prakriti, however, creates *for* the soul and in its vicinity. The atheistic part of Kapila's system was rectified by Patanjala."

In the light of this short extract alone, whose accuracy every student will acknowledge, how gross do RAM CHANDRA's blunders about Kapila appear. Nothing could be more erroneous than to suppose that in the Sankhya system, the element or principle, Purusha, is distinguished as the universal soul, from Prakriti as the particular principle of nature. Kapila recognises no universal Soul; his Purusha is indeed not evolved out of material life, as all else by successive stages is; but it is at the furthest possible remove from Prakriti in its mode of existence and activity, and any real union or relation between them is impossible. The truth is that Kapila's system is only apparently dualistic; it is a disguised Buddhism in rational categories, and an undisguised atheistical Evolutionism in contrast to the universal spiritualism of the Vedantic system. The soul or Purusha, which comes last in the system, is a mere subtle intellectual abstraction which has only a semblance of existence, and is neither produced nor producing. There are many eternal individual souls, something like Plato's ideas, but no supreme, infinite, and eternal Spirit, and the unconscious Prakriti is the only creator, or rather evolver or *procreator*. A Purusha is something quite different and apart from the personal consciousness which is evolved out of nature, and which lives and moves in nature. It is at the most a mere thin, changeless lifeless spectre which once conjured up, it requires all the resources of the system again to lay. I need not dip more deeply into the essence of the Sankhya philosophy here; but it must be already evident that RAM CHANDRA has hardly obtained a glimpse of it.

His misrepresentation of the principle of the Sankhya is only parallelled by the historical absurdity of assigning to Kapila "the glory of first announcing to the world *the profound distinction first made by him between matter and soul*"(!) than which, we are told, "the philosophy of Europe and Asia has not alighted upon a discovery grander, or more fundamental"!! The date of Kapila is still unsettled, and perhaps will never be precisely fixed. But Dr. Banerjea is certainly right in placing him later than Buddhism, and more recent investigations only find him after the Christian era. It may at least be safely maintained that the Sankhya philosophy was not formulated in its technical terms, till long after the greatest pupil of Aristotle carried philosophy with him to India. And will any sciolist, even in the history of philosophy, maintain that "the distinction between matter and soul" was only discovered *then?* It is one of the first distinctions that arise in all human consciousness, even on its lowest stages, and is found everywhere. It was written as with the point of a diamond on the first page of that despised book, the *Bible*, where it still shines with all its deep meaning and bright lustre to-day. It even pervades the Vedas, bursting out in such great hymns as the Purusha Sukta, and the Upanishads laboured to abolish it in vain. Apart from its dominating prominence in Plato and Aristotle, RAM CHANDRA had he been able to consult Böhtlingk and Roth—which I am sure he could not—would have found that even the technical term *Prakriti* was not coined by Kapila, although he may have given it a more philosophical significance and currency. This, indeed, is all that Kapila seems to have done, and I think there is every probability that the philosophical movement in India was largely influenced by the introduction of Greek ideas, and the Sankhya system most of all. There seems to have been a kind of intellectual endosmose and exosmose going on between the East and the West through a very broad and porous diaphragm for centuries, which historical criticism is only begining to explain. The Hindus received some of the first principles of their speculative thinking from the free and progressive Greeks, and they gave them back, steeped in the wild and gross revelling of naturalistic fancy, to the Gnostics and the Neoplatonists of Alexandria. And through these and other point of connection and filiation, we see again how much more competent the European scholars are to "understand and expound" the Hindu systems, than the one-sided and limited Pundits possibly can be. But RAM CHANDRA, it must be admitted, is right *generally,* when he assigns to the Sankhya philosophy a very close and sympathetic relation to the popular idolatry. No one can fail to see this, for the Shivaite and Vishnuite cults are but its theoretical ideas carried out in religious practice. RAM CHANDRA, however, is again all wrong in attributing the three *Gunas,* translate them as he may, to the Purusha rather than to Prakriti; but I shall not pause upon that. His representation of the happy bridal of Nature and the Soul is a little bit of pilfering from modern poetry, which the soul of Kapila would have most deeply abhorred. The view of Kalidasa "soaring above both philosopher and Puranist" is worthy of that most resonant echo of German criticism—Baboo Chunder Nath Bose; but I shall not dwell upon his loftiest type of unholy marriage. The popular idolater may well be proud of Kapila, for in his philosophy he can find a license for all his licentiousness, and a succedaneum for all his superstition. But I cannot return to the filthy subject again, although RAM CHANDRA'S advocacy has only shown more clearly, that it cannot be too fully or too frequently laid bare in all its springs and motives and tendencies. Let this suffice also as illustrative of the statement that "this same distinguished and highly Anglicised native, who must henceforth be prominently immortalised in all histories of Sanskrit literature and Indian thought, has at the same time thoroughly understood the numerous European expositions of the Sankhya system in English, German," &c.

9, 10, 11.—Nor shall I claim space for a discussion of the 9th, 10th, and 11th, articles of RAM CHANDRA'S creed, even if I had time to waste upon them, for it would only be going over again the ground already fully traversed in my discussion of the popular and practical side of the Hindu idolatry. I refer to all I have already written upon the subject, not a word of which, I grieve to say, has yet been shown to be wrong; and I can but too confidently appeal to the consciousness and belief of at least 200 millions of idolaters in India against this iconoclast of all that is nearest and dearest to their faith.

11. I have ventured to characterise his representation of Hinduism "stripped of its rites, its idolatry, its caste," as "a highly philosophical conception." RAM CHANDRA is evidently no nominalist; he must have studied the conceptualism of the Middle Ages, with wonderful success; he might even claim to have soared beyond any European thinker in realising what Hegel calls, "The abstract Universal." So far as the Nineteenth Century can see into it, Hinduism *has only a rotten husk and no kernel.* It is *full of Nothingness,* says Kapila, and all the rest of them, save only RAM CHANDRA. It is vain to try to put life or light or love into its "eyeless socket" again, or to attempt to cover its "rattling bones" with the semblance of new "flesh and blood." Not a breath of real spiritual life stirs in the bare shaking skeleton, and we can now look it through and through. And yet RAM CHANDRA boasts in a last ejaculation of triumph: "I leave *the kernel without the husk,*" although he has forgotten to shew us the *kernel* or even tell us how it looks. The honest Hindu comes off worse than the "navvy," for he at least *had* something to gnaw at;—but this *kernel*! Alas, RAM CHANDRA has only cut through the husk to shew that *his nut is empty.* Apart from "its rites, its idolatry, its caste," there is, indeed, no Hinduism for the Hindu. The Sankhya philosophy was more logical than RAM CHANDRA in declaring "the great duality" unreal, and the union of the soul and nature illegitimate. And hence it would really be of no avail to get a brand-new set of finer looking gods manufactured in Birmingham, even if it should be arranged that their godships should pass like piece-goods through the Custom

House, and that no protective tariff should limit educated Hindus in their more æsthetic worship of the sordid productions of European skill? RAM CHANDRA—let the truth be told—has outlived his Hinduism as much as any of the "anglicised natives" he so thoroughly despises. He is a more abstract thinker than Martinus Scriblerus or even his friend Crambe, who "to show himself of a more penetrating genius, swore that he could frame a conception of a Lord Mayor, not only without his gown and his gold chain, but even without stature, feature, colour, hands, head, feet, or any body, which he supposed was *the abstract* of a Lord Mayor." RAM CHANDRA'S *kernel without the husk*, is just like Martin's *Lord Mayor* without his office and all its belongings and all his qualities. And of Auguste Comte, I shall only say that it is one of the most melancholy and unpromising of my experiences here to be continually reminded that he is "regarded by so many of the Hindus as the profoundest European thinker of the century." Comte has no right to be regarded as a *thinker* in the true sense of the word at all; he was hardly more profound than RAM CHANDRA himself. And on his thirteenth article of belief "that he has expounded or defended *Hinduism*, and that any form of Hinduism *could* survive such exposition and defence," I shall only leave the light that may be reflected from the other twelve to beat as in a focus, and ask any candid critic to judge whether this "thinking" of his is not an "extraordinary hallucination after all."

I have done with what I have to say on this subject in your columns. I hope I have not been too hard upon RAM CHANDRA; if I have been hard at all, it is only because the cause I argue is so much greater than either of us. Almost at the last moment, I have learned that, in accordance with a personal allusion of his own which has made it an open secret, I have had the honour of dealing with one who is indeed honoured by his countrymen as "the Sir Walter Scott of Bengal"—a foeman worthy of *any* steel. Not a leaf would I pluck from his own green garland, but would be fain to point him rather to a "better way," where higher and more enduring laurels may be more easily won. He remembers, no doubt, that humorous scene in his great model, where the amiable and enthusiastic Antiquary, was disillusionised by the plain, matter-of-fact, outspoken Bedesman, so that the Pretorian camp and the glory of old Rome sank into the wreck of a miserable hut, and the mysterious classical symbols A. D. L. L. (which remind us of the mystic OM) turned out to mean nothing more than *Aikin Drum's lang ladle*! It is always unpleasant and trying to the mildest of tempers, to be thus awakened from a golden dream of the past, into the severe strong light of day. But RAM CHANDRA has truly learned that "in the union of the soul with nature lies the source of all beauty, all truth, and all love." But Hinduism did not give him that insight, and far less can it shew him how this union is to be realised as "a legitimate one" and even as "a holy marriage." It has been the blessed prerogative of Christianity alone to teach that truth to mankind; let us beware therefore, lest we throw away the precious *kernel* because we may be foolishly trying to feed upon the *husk*. The example of Sir Walter Scott himself may shew that the reproduction of a romantic past is not the highest in literature, and still less so in religion. Who I ask, in conclusion, is to win the undying fame of opening up to the masses of India, the perennial fountains of poetry, of life, and of hope, that still flow through the crystal currents of Christian Faith ? By such influences "the intellectual inferiority of India," which is but the obverse of his own heading and which I attribute solely and wholly to her idolatry, will soon disappear and her sons will rise again to the highest possibilities of thought and of life. *This* is what the dim eyes and weary hearts of the million of India are looking and hungering for ; and he who will in some measure meet their want, may yet shine "above all Greek, above all Roman fame" and be remembered in the household words of millions yet unborn, when Scotland may have all but forgotten her own romantic bard. Than this I can wish nothing higher for RAM CHANDRA; and this wish I make my closing word of present farewell.

W. HASTIE.

The General Assembly's Institution,
November 1, 1882.

---

## THE RECENT CONTROVERSY.

### TO THE EDITOR.

SIR,—You can easily understand that having spent a whole life on the consideration of the mutual bearing of Christianity and Hinduism on the question of the regeneration of India, I could not have read, without deep interest, the last controversy between Mr. Hastie and our distinguished and accomplished countryman, who appeared under the assumed name of RAM CHANDRA. Now that the controversy has closed, you will perhaps allow me the liberty of a few remarks on the whole subject.

Mr. Hastie, referring to the late Sobha-Bazar *Shrad*, of which you had given an interesting account, with the names of the principal guests, opened fire on such of the guests as having risen above the popular forms of Hinduism, with its idolatrous rites and ceremonies, still encouraged them by their presence. No censure appears to have been pronounced on the *bona fide* performers of the ceremonies, who believed in good faith that they were doing their duty to their deceased common ancestor.

Mr. Hastie's fire was quickly returned with much resoluteness, but the real points in dispute were as speedily ignored. The original charge was levelled against those whom Mr. Hastie took to be disbelievers in idolatry, like himself, but who, unlike himself, encouraged by their presence the celebration of what they believed to be false. I should have thought that under these circumstances there could only be two issues to be argued on—(1) whether the class just defined, was morally wrong in sanctioning and encouraging, by their presence, the performance of rites and ceremonies in which they had no faith whatever; and (2) whether the gentlemen whom Mr. Hastie had singled out by name all belonged to the condemned class.

These, the real issues of the question, were scarcely touched in the controversy that has now closed. In fact they were almost entirely forgotten in the concluding letter of RAM CHANDRA, which, again, unconsciously to the writer, contained views and terms fully justifying the charge with which Mr. Hastie had commenced the controversy.

RAM CHANDRA has called the idolatrous rites and ceremonies of Hinduism its *husks*, not its *kernel*. Mr. Hastie censured those guests who might be of the same opinion as RAM CHANDRA (and their name would be *legion* according to your correspondent), with wrongly encouraging, by their presence, the *chewing* of those very husks, instead of their *eschewing*. Your talented correspondent has himself given a good instance, in point, of the *injuriousness* of such *chewing*. A navvy had strayed into the country, and was impelled by his hunger to ask a native for some food. A cocoanut was given him, with instructions how to take it. The foreign griff was too hungry to listen to those instructions, and at once began to *chew the husk*, which no doubt materially injured his teeth and gums. Suppose the donor of the fruit had given no instrucions, but on the contrary had encouraged him *to go on chew-*

*ing*, would not the unfeeling man be held responsible for the sufferings of the poor sailor? If RAM CHANDRA'S view of Hinduism be right, then, on his own theory, Mr. Hastie could not be wrong in condemning and denouncing those persons who were inflicting serious injury, from a moral point of view, on their hosts and neighbours by encouraging *husk-chewing.*

As to the view of Hinduism which RAM CHANDRA has propounded, I am obliged to confess to a sad feeling of disappointment. Whatever the pen of the author of "Kapala Kundala" offers to the public, is entitled to our patient attention. But what can be more startling; what more galling to our national pride; what more opposed to our early intuitions, and our unwritten traditions of past ages, than the unequivocal denial of the Vedas ("which are dead!") as the authoritative basis of Hinduism. This denial flatly contradicts Manu and all the authors of our sacred literature; nay, pours contempt on the whole civilized world. All quarters of the globe had welcomed Max Müller's edition of the *Rigveda* as the restoration of India's long-lost treasury of literature and of theology. The late Raja Radhakant, rigidly orthodox as he was, called the Mlecha editor a second Veda-restoring *Avatar.* Pundits had complimented him by reading his name as "MOX-MULL," or the *root of salvation.* All India has congratulated itself on the printing and publishing of her most valued sacred literature, and yet RAM CHANDRA casts the Vedas away to the moles and to the bats! But a *living* work which has already passed through many editions cannot now be cast away as dead! It would be like consigning a living man to the earth, and burying him alive.

It is difficult to say what your correspondent's idea of Hindu *Philosophy* is. He has certainly extolled the Sankhya and the Nyaya. But Kapila could not allow the creative agency of *Purusha,* and the *Nyaya* could never be so disloyal to its Atoms as to allow any place for *Prakriti.* The schools of philosophy could not be impressed to our new religion-maker's aid unless they were mutilated by the strain of his pulls.

Without mentioning any *inventor*, he speaks of a "bold eclecticism" which gave rise to the beautiful religion, which, says he, "I do not believe to be of divine origin, but which I accept as the perfection of human wisdom." Such respect is due to RAM CHANDRA, but before we can receive this new system of October 1882, as an *ipse dixit,* we may be compelled to appeal to the author of Kapala Kundala, and consider what HIS *ipse dixit* is.

RAM CHANDRA tells us that "nothing has so largely influenced the fate of some of the Indian peoples as the *Tantras*, and of Tantra literature the European knows next to nothing." If this has any meaning, it must be that the *Tantra* with its *unwritten traditions,* is the general basis of the Hindu religion, and, consistently enough, he maintains that the Hindu worships the "illicit union" between Purusha and Prakriti, retained in the "illegitimate connection of Krishna and Radha." As a reader of Kapala Kundala, I am amazed at such statements.

I believe that there are many Hindus who, inclining to the Vedant, and looking for the *Mukti* which it promises, have nothing to say to Prakriti, while even of those who do speak of Purusha and Prakriti, the vast majority is innocent of the worship of any "illicit union." If there be worshippers and imitators of "illicit unions," they must chiefly be in circles of Mohunts and recluse hermits, whether of the Vaishnava or Sakteya sects. Householders, men of repute in society, the better classes of the Hindu community, cannot and could not be included in such secret circles. It would be a cruel defamation of Hindu families to attribute to them belief in the system elaborated by RAM CHANDRA from Tantric sources. The followers of Nyaya, Vedant and Sankhya philosophies would repudiate such an abuse of the ideas of Purusha and Prakriti, and the best practical *exposé* of the "illicit union" is contained in that great Bengali romance, the *Kapala Kundala.* The great Tantric hero of that inimitable novel is Kapalic, a representative worshipper of Bhavani and Bhoiravi, as personations of Sakti or Prakriti. This man is described as an eremite far from towns and villages, adopting and fostering foundling girls, only to dishonour them when they grow up, and waylaying and decoying benighted young men, only to sacrifice them before the shrine of his goddess, *because* the Tantric cannot accomplish his worship without human flesh, and *because,* without violating the chastity of women, the Tantric cannot attain perfection. Those allegations in the Kapala Kundala are fully justified by passages contained in the Tantras. We sometimes come across other evidences of such nefarious practices in courts of justice, both in criminal and civil cases. A few years ago, all India was startled by reports of a case of the "Maharajas" (spiritual preceptors) in the Western Presidency. They confessed without a blush that as they were personations of Krishna, women sought with gifts of money to attain to divinity like Radha, by illicit connexion with them, and this was Tantric perfection! In our own province, the case of the Mohunt of Tarkeswar is still fresh in our memories.

To one more evidence I must draw attention. Not many years ago the late Kalidas Sing of sterling honesty as an author, wrote a book in Bengali, called "Hutam-pancha," in which he exposed many evils in religious sects, and, among others, the practice of the guru prasadias, which was not to let a bridegroom approach his bride, before the guru had first consecrated her by carnal knowledge!

Such is the Tantric system. It revels in luxury in forests and other recesses, away from towns and villages.

Let it never be misnamed as the general religion

of the Hindus, nor let the Hindus be exhorted to adopt such a Tantric system with all its filthiness.

What, then, it may be asked is the general religion of the Hindus? I can only answer the question by the help of our past written literature, including the "*dead Vedas*." No Hinduism can be found any where that will correspond to every age and epoch in the history of the Hindus. I think it has passed through four stages from the commencement, and without further preface, I will at once say a few words on its passage through those stages,

I.—The first or primitive stage of Hinduism is marked by the celebration of sacrificial rites, as figures or images of Prajapati, the Lord of the Creation, who "had offered himself a sacrifice for emancipated souls" (*Satapatha Brahmana*). The same Prajapati is elsewhere described as the Purusha, "begotten from the beginning," whom "the gods sacrificed on the sacred grass." This sacrifice, the figure of Prajapati, was a "good ferrying-boat for getting over the ocean of sins." I speak of this doctrine as I find it in my living guide—the Vedas. From this doctrine, our primitive ancestors had obtained a prospect of Futurity, with which no ideal of *metempsychosis* can vie—and they derived a comfort of which no one who does not understand how *death has been vanquished*, can have any notion. Witness the language of the believing sacrificer addressed to a dying father; "Proceed, proceed, my father, to that place where your faithful precursors have gone before—there, laying down your sinful body, be endued with a glorious body." Of this doctrine, then, and of its consequent practice of sacrifices—involving, as they do, the acknowledgment of a "Lord of the Creation," the father of *gods* and *asuras*—no Hindu can be ashamed. He may, on the contrary, take a just pride in that they contained germs, the legitimate development of which is now found in the faith of the most civilized portions of humanity.

II.—The second stage was characterized by a change from the monotheistic to the dualistic in doctrine, but the practice of sacrifices continued as before. The dualistic consisted in the acknowledgment of the Zoroastrian Ahur-Mazdu and Angro-Mainus. The first was Sanskritized Asura-pracheta, or Asura viswaveda, and the latter Nirrit, the two Sanskrit names bearing respectively the same meaning as the two Zend appellatives. A declension in doctrine rapidly followed. The self-offering of Prajapati was forgotten, and the significance of sacrifice as a figure of Prajapati was also lost. Sacrificial rites and ceremonies, however still continued, and with greater frequency, under innumerable forms and symbols. But the true doctrine being lost, those ceremonies degenerate into objectless and wanton acts of bloodshed, which in time led to that terrific assault of Buddhism, which, when Brahminism got its final triumph, still left strong traces, partly visible to this day. And this leads me to the third or post-Buddhic stage of Hinduism.

III.—At this stage it was that philosophy began to influence the creeds of India. The Nyaya, while it contended for Brahminical supremacy, generally adopted the grounds on which Buddhism had based its doctrine of Renunciation and Nirvan. The Nyaya did not follow the principles of Sakya Singha in his description of the world as a *maya* or *mirage*, but it proclaimed the doctrine of Mukti as the final consummation of Hinduism. The Sankhya, with greater Buddhistic tendency, denied the existence of an Intelligent Creator, and pointed to a final consummation not unlike that of Buddhism. The Vedanta, though decidedly an advocate for the Veda and the dignity of the Brahminhood, yet inculcated the idea of a final absorption in Brahma, which is also called Nirvan. But the subtleties of dialectics could not satisfy the popular mind. Jaimini came forward with his Mimansa for the restoration of the old ceremonies. The end of the Vedas, he says, was *works*; "nothing could be of any avail which aimed at other ends". Although this gave to the third stage a somewhat longer lease of life, yet another stage followed eventually, of which personal religion and personal faith were the chief characteristics.

IV.—I shall not stop here to consider whether this stage was the product entirely of Hindu thought, or whether it was brought about by incidents outside India. I shall leave RAM CHANDRA to settle this point with one of the European giants of Sanskrit literature, who needed no champions, and whom he has introduced to us by name. I allude to Professor Weber. I shall only add that in this stage Krishna was invested with supreme divinity, at the head of the Pantheon, not, however, without occasional conflicts with Siva, who aspired after the same dignity. Sects or religious fraternities were established, having, for their *Ishta devata*, or peculiar object of worship, either Krishna, Siva, or Sakti. Persons who joined those sects were generally called "Bhactas," though there were many families of similar persuasions who lived as seculars and laymen. And there still remained a large residuum which, without joining any particular fraternity, continued in the performance of caste duties.

Although somewhat coloured by lapse of time and considerably affected by foreign rule, yet the same stage continues to this day. The general body of Hindus live like seculars, supporting and maintaining those to whose care the *arcana* of their faith were consigned, and themselves keeping up religious demonstrations by means of their several costly poojahs. The Bráhmin, however, is still bound to daily repetitions of the Gayatri and Sandhya, the former being a Vedic verse, and the latter a collection of Vedic passages, but neither are in any way connected with the Tantras. He is also bound to the worship of Vishnu and Siva, without any reference to Purusha or Prakriti.

It is not necessary to say more. I conclude with

declaring that I perfectly agree with the Hindu gentleman who said to a European missionary at Benares : " You know we have properly no longer any religious belief: every one may believe what he likes, if he will only observe the rules of caste. " (*Christlieb, p. 51.*)

K. M. BANERJEA.

November 10, 1882.

---

## XX. THE RECENT CONTROVERSY.

### To the Editor.

Sir,—I have no wish to re-open the controversy I have closed, but allow me to remove a misconception—a most painful one, as your readers will see.

Dr. K. M. Banerjee writes :—"Ram Chanda tells us that nothing has so largely influenced the fate of some of the Indian peoples as the *Tantras*, and of the *Tantra* literature the European knows next to nothing. If this has any meaning, it must be that the *Tantra* with its *unwritten traditions*, is the general basis of Hinduism."

That certainly is *not* the meaning, and I have not understood how sueh an interpretation has been arrived at. There may be opinions which influence the destinies of nations, without being the base of national religion. The paganism of Greece has largely moulded, in some of its aspects at least, the civilisation of modern Europe ; but the paganism of ancient Greece is not the general basis of Christianity. Islamism has very greatly influenced the destinies of India, without being the general basis of Hinduism. Christianity at this day largely influences the destinies of India, yet Christianity is not the general basis of Hinduism.

What the influence of Tantrikism has been on the people of Bengal, of Assam, and of Orissa, I do not propose to discuss here. I do not say that the influence has been beneficial. I can assure Dr. Banerjee that he cannot be more emphatic in the condemnation of Tantrikism than I am, and that I have in no respect departed from the view I put forth and illustrated in *Kapala Kundala* in regard to the morality of that form of Hinduism. True Hinduism and Tantrikism are as much opposed to each other as light and darkness, and I say with as much sincerity as he does, that let it never be assumed that Tantrikism is the general religion of the Hindus; no one, I believe, has ever thought of making such an assumption.

Let Tantrikism perish—but let it not perish unstudied. The study of the darkest errors of humanity yields lessons as valuable as that of Truth itself. And what is history, if it is not the history of human errors.

When Mr. Hastie talked of the "Tantrika Bible," and such other nonsense, I did not consider it necessary to make a reply: he had shown himself not to be entitled to any. It is different when Dr. Bannerjee misconceives my meaning. I respect him too highly to remain silent.

As it can no longer be necessary to write under an assumed name, I subscribe my own.

BANKIM CHUNDER CHATTERJEE.

November 18, 1882.

NOTE.—This must terminate the controversy.—ED., S. (To which note, in the meantime, I subscribe.—W. H.)

JUST READY, FOURTH THOUSAND. PRICE ONE RUPEE.

# PROTESTANT MISSIONS TO THE HEATHEN:

A Survey of their recent Progress and present State throughout the World.

By Dr. TH. CHRISTLIEB, *Professor of Theology at Bonn.*

Translated from the German, with Additions and Appendices,

By W. HASTIE, B. D.

*Principal of the General Assembly's Institution, Calcutta.*

NOTE—This little work contains a general Survey of the Protestant Missions throughout the world, with full Statistics drawn from the most recent authorities. It is universally acknowledged to be the best representation of the work of the Protestant Missions at Present. This Edition, which is Published with the sanction of the Author, has been prepared on the basis of two private Editions which have been sent to Scotland and England within a few months. The Author writing lately to the Translator says, "I was greatly surprised to see the *third* English Translation—all of them done by Presbyterians . . . Yours is more free than the others, but you catch the thought or the substance of it in its true meaning. Your statistical addition is very valuable. The Lord has granted much blessing on this labor to 4 German, 3 English, 3 American, 2 Indian Editions (I have received the proof of your Second Edition) ; then a French translation, a Norwegian, etc. Even from Japan, I received letters of thanks." Any profit derived from the sale of this Edition, will be devoted to the work of the Church of Scotland Mission at Govindpore in Manbhoom.